ACCLAIM FOR

The
TINNED FISH
COOKBOOK

An Amazon Best Book of the Month—Cookbooks, Food & Wine

"Bart van Olphen elevates canned tuna to the heights of deliciousness."
—The New York Times

"*The Tinned Fish Cookbook* [has] simple, tasty recipes that celebrate and elevate the humble canned fish from an overlooked back-of-the-pantry ingredient to one that deserves center stage."**—Food & Wine**

"For the ardent sustainable eater or the seafood fanatic trying to rein in the swordfish eating in favor of cheaper, better-for-the-planet fish, this tiny little book is a perfect (and adorable) guide."**—Epicurious**

"A lot of [us] don't really know what to do with all those cans of sardines and mackerel . . . along comes [this] little book."**—Esquire**

"[For] enjoying the ocean in your pantry. . . . Far from a fallback, canned fish deserves our respect."**—National Post**

"[*The Tinned Fish Cookbook*] realizes the potential of canned seafood with 45 recipes for tuna, mackerel, herring, and mussels."
—Publishers Weekly

"Bart is my fish hero . . . I'm off to buy some tinned fish!"**—Jamie Oliver**

Rien,

*This book is dedicated to you, in memory of an intensely beautiful
friendship. Ever since we met in the kitchen at catering school, we spent
time together cooking, eating, laughing, and living. Always spontaneously,
on the spur of the moment. That's how it was. That's how we rolled.
From The Hague to Paris, from Amsterdam to Barcelona. And then
suddenly you were gone. But you'll never be gone from my heart.
Thank you, buddy! Love you!*

Richard de Nijs

December 6, 1969–October 8, 2017

The
TINNED FISH
COOKBOOK

Easy-to-Make Meals from Ocean to Plate
Sustainably Canned, 100% Delicious

BART VAN OLPHEN
Photos by DAVID LOFTUS

THE EXPERIMENT

NEW YORK

The Experiment, LLC
220 East 23rd Street, Suite 600
New York, NY 10010-4658
theexperimentpublishing.com

THE EXPERIMENT and its colophon are registered trademarks of The Experiment, LLC. Many of the designations used by manufacturers and sellers to distinguish their products are claimed as trademarks. Where those designations appear in this book and The Experiment was aware of a trademark claim, the designations have been capitalized.

The Experiment's books are available at special discounts when purchased in bulk for premiums and sales promotions as well as for fund-raising or educational use. For details, contact us at info@theexperimentpublishing.com.

Library of Congress Cataloging-in-Publication Data

Names: Van Olphen, Bart, author. | Loftus, David, photographer. | Vroomen,
  Laura, translator.
Title: The tinned fish cookbook : easy-to-make meals from ocean to plate—sustainably canned,
  100% delicious / Bart van Olphen ; photos by David Loftus ; translation by Laura Vroomen.
Other titles: Vis uit blik 2. English
Description: New York : The experiment, 2020. | Originally published in the
  Netherlands as Vis uit blik 2 by Kosmos Uitgevers in 2019.
Identifiers: LCCN 2019054651 (print) | LCCN 2019054652 (ebook) | ISBN
  9781615196746 (hardcover) | ISBN 9781615196753 (ebook)
Subjects: LCSH: Cooking (Fish) | Cooking (Seafood) | Cooking (Canned foods)
  | LCGFT: Cookbooks.
Classification: LCC TX747 .V32513 2020 (print) | LCC TX747 (ebook) | DDC
  641.3/92--dc23
LC record available at https://lccn.loc.gov/2019054651
LC ebook record available at https://lccn.loc.gov/2019054652

ISBN 978-1-61519-674-6
Ebook ISBN 978-1-61519-675-3

Cover design by Beth Bugler and Jack Dunnington
Text design and illustrations by Tijs Koelemeijer
Culinary editing by Lars Hamer
Food styling and production by Inge Tichelaar
Original Dutch edition text and editing by Eline Cox
Translation by Laura Vroomen

Manufactured in China

First printing May 2020
10 9 8 7 6 5 4 3 2

Note: The tablespoons used in this book have a standard volume of 0.5 fluid ounces (15 ml), teaspoons ⅙ fluid ounce (5 ml). Spoons are always level, unless otherwise indicated.

CONTENTS

INTRODUCTION

It was around fifteen years ago that I fell in love with tinned fish as I traveled through countries like Spain, Portugal, and France, where they really know and adore it. Aside from the lovely packaging of many of these tins—reason enough to buy them—the fish inside was surprisingly flavorsome, too. I remember visiting a small-scale *conserverie*, or cannery, in northern Brittany during those years. Just before I left, the owner, Marie Bevillon, handed me a gorgeous tin of sardines. "Don't eat it right away!" she said. "Turn it over regularly and they'll get even better, like a good bottle of wine." And they did! I've been sold ever since.

My passion for fish began in the mid-1990s. With the Michelin Guide and my catering school diploma under my arm, I boarded the train to Paris. Since early childhood it had been my big dream to work at a Michelin three-star restaurant. I was given my first taste of this at Lucas Carton, one of the top gourmet restaurants in Paris. I started off washing lettuce and peeling potatoes, but soon found myself preparing the starters and mains—including many different kinds of fish, all with their own unique flavor and texture. Here I learned that preparing fish is actually really simple, and that you can put a terrific fish course on the table in just a few steps.

My learning experience in France got me hooked on creating and preparing all kinds of fish dishes—fast-forward years later, and now I'm just as happy preparing a recipe with a tin as I am using a piece of fresh fish. That's because tinned fish is surprisingly versatile in the kitchen. But it calls for preparation with a slightly different mind-set, since the fish has already been cooked inside the tin. It's a question of combining flavors, adding a drop of acidity, a touch of color, and a bit of crunch. But the best thing about cooking with tinned fish is that it's simple, quick, and absolutely delicious!

Unlike its fresh and frozen counterparts, the fish that goes into tins is almost all caught in the wild, and much of it is oily fish—many people's favorite—which lends itself particularly well to canning. Tuna, salmon, sardines, anchovy, and mackerel in water or oil taste sensational. Often, the fish is caught in peak season, too, which is beneficial for both fish stocks and quality: It guarantees you'll get the most succulent fish at an affordable price, thanks to the efficient production processes. Not to mention the tins usually have an unrefrigerated shelf life of over four years, so you never have to worry about it rotting in your fridge.

But not all tinned fish is created equal. I have traveled extensively to fish, cook, and live with the most amazing and responsible fishing communities all over the world, and I've learned it's important to know where our fish comes from and how it was caught. More than 80 percent of the world's oceans are currently fished to capacity or are overfished, so when you buy fish, make sure it's from sustainable stocks. Thankfully, the labels on tins inform consumers whether the fish comes from a sustainable (certified) fishery. (As you'll learn, MSC certification is best.) Transparency makes all the difference. That's why this book doesn't just contain scrumptious recipes, but also introduces you to the fishermen and women who ensure that you can continue to enjoy the tastiest fish with a clear conscience.

It has been my joy and privilege to compile over forty recipes using the various kinds of tinned fish available in stores so you can enjoy the best that they have to offer: recipes for a quick bite, snacks, appetizers, lunch, and dinner that incorporate a delightful range of tinned fish—from tuna to mackerel to herring and more. Many of them are easy, fast, affordable, and, above all, fun to make. And though the recipes serve two people, if you're catering to a bigger household, note that you can simply multiply the ingredients to create your fishy feast.

I hope this book will inspire you to regularly use tinned fish in the kitchen—sustainably caught and exceedingly delicious, of course. Enjoy!

COOKING WITH CANS

Think tasty fish, and you'll probably think of smoked salmon or a fried cod fillet. But did you know that a lot of wild fish for consumption is canned? The quality of tinned fish is in no way inferior to that of fresh fish, since the original product is identical. But the preservation process does alter both taste and texture, just as it prolongs shelf life. And the latter is not just incredibly handy, but also very sustainable. If you always keep a few tins of fish on hand, you can put a delicious meal on the table in no time!

A TINNED HISTORY OF FISH

It was in the mid-1800s that products were first preserved in glass, and soon after in cans, too, in an effort to prevent fresh foodstuffs—including fish—from spoiling. But canned food didn't really catch on until the next century, during the two world wars. During the First World War, millions of troops ate food from tins in the trenches.

Over the years, modern production techniques, changing materials, and other innovations have increased the shelf life and overall quality of tinned food. Demand rose rapidly from the late 1960s onward, when more and more women went out to work and cans were marketed as a convenience product. People discovered that canned food not only saved the modern woman time, but it could be pretty tasty, too.

CATCH OF THE DAY

With current canning techniques it's possible to preserve fish for up to five years. This bodes well for the future: a surplus of fish that's brought in can be canned so it doesn't go to waste. This is a great way to combat food loss, and it's equally important to realize that the use of tin is sustainable in itself. The material is easily separated by waste processors and can be recycled again and again. Add to that the fact that tinned fish is always caught in peak season and is often reasonably priced, and you have an amazing product—flavorful, affordable, and with a long shelf life!

FISH IS THE FUTURE

To guarantee that we can keep catching, conserving, and consuming fish in the future, it's important that we only opt for sustainably caught fish—fish from fisheries that use appropriate techniques and catch no more than is environmentally responsible. This gives less healthy fish stocks the chance to recover.

While it can sometimes be a challenge to establish where fresh fish is from and how it was caught, the label on a tin can gives us all the information we need as consumers. Thanks to transparency about the types of fish processed, fishing methods, and provenance, it's easy for fish lovers to make the right choice. The Marine Stewardship Council—the leading third-party certification program—provides further clarity with its sustainable certification scheme. The MSC label is the most reliable ecolabel for sustainably caught wild fish, and for me it's the only gold standard in some cases. When it comes to tuna, we should only consume certified fish caught by pole and line. Following the guidelines of the Monterey Bay Aquarium Seafood Watch is a good and reliable reference, but the best way to go is the MSC, as they trace every seafood product back to the source by chain of custody principles. Simply put: Buy a product that is MSC-certified *and* caught by pole and line, and you know you can enjoy your seafood with good conscience. More information about the MSC can be found on p. 16.

ONE MORE TIN

One final thing to note about fish in a tin—you may come across three labels: "No Salt Added," "Non-GMO," and "BPA-Free."

"No Salt Added" Since fish often comes from salty water, you can't get it completely without salt, but most brands also provide no salt added options for those who have to be careful about their sodium intake. If this is you, keep it in mind!

"Non-GMO" There's only one GMO fish currently available for consumption in the US, so when brands label their tins "non-GMO" it's just to reassure increasingly health-conscious consumers that the fish within is in no way genetically modified. But since all fish is caught in the wild (often advertised on the can as "wild caught"), you can rest assured the fish is non-GMO even without the label (though not necessarily sustainable!).

"BPA-Free" About 90 percent of canned foods no longer contain BPA in their linings, but it still can be found in some tins. If you see the "BPA-Free" label, this is just another reassurance to health-conscious consumers: It's worth noting that the FDA, based on hundreds of studies, has found that the low levels of BPA found in food is safe.

TO A BOIL

Ask people what dishes they prepare with tinned fish and chances are they'll come up with just a handful of recipes. Ingenious cooking with tinned fish calls for some basic knowledge. One important thing to know is that the fish that goes into a tin is heated to a high temperature. "So what?" you may ask. It means, quite simply, that the fish has already been prepared for you and there's no need to cook it through again.

The canning process changes the taste as well as the color, and the flesh is softer than that of fresh fish. This is worth bearing in mind when cooking with tinned fish. All you need to do to create an appetizing dish is add color, herbs and spices, some acidity, and texture. It's a bit like doing a jigsaw puzzle: Fit the right pieces together and the result is a delicious, well-balanced meal.

IN WATER OR IN OIL?

There you are in the supermarket, overwhelmed at the sight of all those different varieties of tinned fish on the shelves. In water, all kinds of oil, sauces . . . which one to get? Here's a good rule of thumb for when you're going to cook with tinned fish: The variety preserved in water lends itself particularly well to cold dishes with oil added later. Think of a salad with vinaigrette or a spoonful of mayo. Fish in water dries out faster when it's heated, which does not benefit the flavor.

Fish preserved in oil works great in hot dishes. It really comes into its own when you add fresh flavorings—citrus, capers, and green herbs. And if it's of good quality, you can use the oil in the rest of the recipe. Once opened, fish from a tin will keep for 2 to 3 days in the fridge.

If you prefer to eat your tinned fish on its own, but do want to eat it warm, you can place the can in boiling water for 2 minutes.

SAN DIEGO, CALIFORNIA
JACK
FISH TALES

" Together with my colleagues from the AAFA (American Albacore Fishing
Association) I fish for delicious Albacore tuna down the American west coast.
In 2006 we were the first MSC certified tuna fishery in the world, something
we are very proud of. From my boat, the Willie G, we use the traditional fishing
rod method, catching the tuna fish by fish, one by one. " -Jack

32°42'54"-N --- 117°9'45"-W

FISH TALES

ALBACORE
WILD TUNA
IN WATER   WITH A TOUCH OF SEA SALT

100%
POLE & LINE

FISH TALES
PILCHARD
SARDINES
IN OLIVE OIL

ALBACORE
WILD TUNA
IN OLIVE OIL

FISH TALES

ANCHOVY FILLETS

FISH TALES
ANCHOVY
FILLETS

IN OLIVE OIL

NET WT 1.6 OZ (45g)
DR WT 0.8 OZ (22g)

100%
POLE & LINE

CERTIFIED
SUSTAINABLE
SEAFOOD
MSC
www.msc.org

NON
GMO
VERIFIED

Nutrition
Facts

TRACEABLE FROM SEA TO PLATE

SKIPJACK
WILD TUNA
IN WATER   NO SALT ADDED

100%
POLE & LINE

SARDINES
water

FISH TALES
SARDINES
IN WATER

SARDINES
WATER

CANNED OR JARRED?

Besides the tins we love to cook with, fish is also preserved in glass jars. How do they differ? Let's illustrate this with a look at herring. Unlike its canned counterpart, herring from a jar is not heated, but is cured and pickled instead. The fish is marinated to prolong its shelf life. Think of matjes herring and rollmops, which are perfect in dishes like Potato and Herring Salad (p. 127).

The herring destined for jars is sorted and filleted straight after being caught. The fillets are placed in a mixture of water, salt, and vinegar before being stored. The fish then undergoes a ripening process that—depending on the end product—takes thirty to seventy days. This not only prolongs the herring's shelf life, but also gives it its unique flavor.

Depending on demand, the herring is packed year-round with a blend of seasonings that gives the product its distinctive flavor. The herring keeps for ten to twenty weeks—shorter than tinned, but a lot longer than fresh fish. Jarred herring can be found in the refrigerated sections of stores.

And then there's fish in a pouch: There's really no difference between it and tinned fish. It's just another way of packaging that's perhaps easier to use, though a tin is undeniably sturdier—and better looking, too!

THE SUSTAINABLE CHOICE

Enjoying fish with a clear conscience—it seems a tall order, yet it's anything but. If you're after a sustainable fish product, you should buy only fish with the MSC or ASC label. MSC is the certification for wild fish, ASC for farmed fish. At present, both wild and farm-raised fish are processed and canned in the US, but MSC- and ASC-certified brands from all over the world are available in stores, too.

If you want to eat tuna with confidence, it is also important to opt for the pole-and-line caught variety. Pole and line is the only sustainable method of fishing for tuna. It avoids any bycatch and damage to the environment and other marine creatures. It's also far more lucrative for the fishermen than going out in big boats and scooping tuna out of the water with nets. You can read more about the socioeconomic advantages on p. 18. Besides MSC certification and pole-and-line caught methods, other "sustainability labels"—they're all over the packaging these days—offer no guarantee whatsoever. Just think of the meaningless phrase "dolphin-friendly" or the self-proclaimed "responsible catch." Don't be fooled.

WHAT'S THE ROLE OF THE MARINE STEWARDSHIP COUNCIL?

MSC (with its easily recognizable blue label) stands for Marine Stewardship Council. This nonprofit organization has developed an internationally recognized ecolabeling and certification program aimed at protecting our oceans. To qualify for certification, a fishery must meet the MSC standards for sustainably caught fish. These are the strictest and most comprehensive standards for wild seafood fisheries. Once a fishery is awarded the certificate, it can expect annual inspections. And every five years a complete reassessment is carried out to see whether the fishery still complies with the standards and continues to honor its commitments. If you're curious to see which criteria a fishery must meet, just visit msc.org.

WHAT DOES THE
FISHERMAN NET?

A fisherman nets fish, Obviously. But what does the fisherman net for that fish? While it's important that fish is caught sustainably from healthy stocks, we should also consider the well-being of the entire fishing community.

According to the Food and Agriculture Organization of the United Nations, no less than 10 to 12 percent of the total world population depends directly or indirectly on fishing. Of that number, 90 percent work in small-scale fishing communities. Nearly all of these people (97 percent live in developing countries (The World Bank, 2012). A total of 3.7 million fishing vessels ply the world's oceans and "only" 1.7 percent of these can be classified as large-scale. This may seem like a tiny percentage until we realize that these large boats are responsible for 60 percent of the global fish catch (World Ocean Observatory, 2017). With our support, small-scale fishing communities—and all those who depend on fishing for their livelihoods—can continue their sustainable working methods.

THE MALDIVES MODEL

Laamu Atoll, an island that's part of the Maldives, is home to Horizon Fisheries. For decades, this small atoll community has fished for tuna using the authentic pole-and-line method. In fact, it's an integral part of its culture. You can read more about the fishery and its methods on p. 24.

Pole and line is a very labor-intensive method, requiring lots of manual work and thus creating employment for the local population. By eating the tuna caught by companies like Horizon, we contribute not only to the health of our oceans, but also to the livelihood of the fishermen and their families. Fishing has traditionally been their principal source of income.

TUNA

SPECIES
Skipjack tuna (Katsuwonus pelamis)
Albacore tuna (Thunnus alalunga)

AVERAGE WEIGHT AND LENGTH
Skipjack (or striped tuna): 11 pounds, 2 feet
    3 inches long (5 kg and 70 cm)
Albacore (or white tuna): 66 pounds, 3 feet
    7 inches long (30 kg and 110 cm)

FISHING METHODS
Pole and line, seine nets

**SOME MSC-CERTIFIED POLE-AND-LINE
TUNA FISHERIES**
Horizon Fisheries on Laamu Atoll, the Maldives
    (skipjack)
American Albacore Fishing Association in San
    Diego, California (albacore)
North Atlantic Albacore Artisanal Fishery in
    Hondarribia, Spain (albacore)
Meiho Fishery in Shiogama, Japan (skipjack
    and albacore)

BOBBING AROUND ON A DHONI

Pole-and-line fishing is the only method used by the tuna fishers in the Maldives. It's native to their culture. Having fished this way for centuries, they have become one with the ecosystem: one hook, one line, one fisherman, one fish caught at a time.

On Laamu Atoll, a group of tuna fishermen from Horizon Fisheries will gather every day at dusk. As the last light of the day fades, they set sail in a *dhoni,* the region's traditional fishing vessel. Around ten o'clock in the evening, once the boat has anchored, some fifteen fishermen will be lying on deck. The temperature will be quite pleasant, in the mid-eighties. It does not get much hotter or colder around here, close to the equator. The fishermen pass the time with a card game, a chat, or a bite to eat. They're waiting for their nets to fill with small fish—the fish that the skipjack tuna feed on and that will be used as bait when the sun rises. Several hours later, when the captain has decided there's enough bait, he will start the engine and sail farther out on the Indian Ocean.

The sun is rising rapidly now, which is the signal for the crew to pick up their poles. At the back of the boat the sprinklers are switched on, so the moving water hides the azure-colored dhoni from the tuna. The fishermen spread out across the deck. Like the players on a soccer team lining up for a match, everybody knows his position.

And then the spectacle kicks off. Two men scoop a basket of bait out of a basin and toss it into the water. Because the boat is slowly moving forward, the fish feed ends up behind the stern, where the tuna are then lifted out of the water, one at a time. Every ten minutes, or whenever the deck is full of fish, the tuna is put on ice in the hold—ready to be processed and canned within the space of a few hours.

At the point of catch, it's one hook, one line, one fisherman, one fish. But because each boat has some ten to fifteen fishermen, the total they bring in is often substantial.

Every night, several boats set sail from Laamu Atoll on behalf of Horizon Fisheries. An average catch will yield 6,600 pounds (3,000 kg) of skipjack per boat. A simple calculation tells us that if 50 percent of the fish is left after filleting and 3.5 ounces (100 g) of tuna go into one tin, you end up with some 15,000 tins. This result, multiplied by several boats, provides the local fishing community with a good source of income—and provides people all over the world with delicious tinned fish.

WHITE OR STRIPED?

Tuna can be found in all shapes and sizes in oceans across the world. The four species that are most common for consumption are skipjack, albacore, bigeye, yellowfin, and bluefin. The first three tend to find their way into our beloved tins, but yellowfin is often uncertified, and so not recommended.

Skipjack, a predator that swims in large schools of thousands of fish, is found mainly in regions around the equator. Albacore prefers a subtropical climate and eats other shoal fish, including sardines, small mackerel, and anchovies. They can move at speeds of up to 50 miles (80 km) per hour.

WE ALL LOVE TUNA!

Worldwide, tuna is one of the most popular fish for consumption. This is not surprising, given its delicious taste and excellent texture. In food cultures around the world, the oily fish is prepared in distinctive ways. In Japan, for example, the preparation of sashimi has been elevated to an art form, while in Peru they know exactly how to cook tuna in citrus juice for the perfect ceviche, and in the Maldives they use tinned tuna as the basis for what may well be the best tuna salad in the world: *mas huni* (p. 33).

When you cook with tinned tuna—or tinned fish in general—it's worth remembering that the variety in water is ideal for cold dishes and the one in oil for hot food. So prepare Pasta Puttanesca (p. 38) and Thai Tuna Red Curry (p. 49) with tuna in oil, but use tuna in water for the mas huni.

THE RIGHT FISH

All around the world, tuna stocks are under pressure. You can determine whether it's responsible to eat tuna depending on the region where a particular variety is caught or on the fishing method that's used. Choosing the right tuna is not as complicated as you think! Make sure the tin features the MSC-certified label and is guaranteed pole-and-line caught and you can enjoy your fish with a clear conscience. For more information, see p. 16.

Now, before you get started, one final note about tinned fish: These recipes call out the net weight for each tin of fish (e.g., "one 6-ounce [160 g] tin of tuna"). This is normally listed on the front of the tin, and is different from the drained weight (what the fish weighs without the oil or water inside the tin). Some tins may list the drained weight, others may not, but just remember: The net weight is what we're working with.

TUNA MELT WITH KETCHUP
›SERVES 2 FOR LUNCH OR A SNACK‹

This seemingly simple toasted sandwich with tuna and lots of cheese is a real American classic. Why? The proof is in the eating.

TUNA MELT

One 6-ounce (160 g) tin of tuna in sunflower oil, drained
1 small red onion, diced
1 scallion, white and light green parts, finely chopped
¼ bunch of flat-leaf parsley, leaves only, coarsely chopped
3 tablespoons mayonnaise
Tabasco sauce
4 slices of bread, preferably rustic
1½ tablespoon (20 g) butter
4 slices of cheddar cheese

Salt and pepper, to taste

KETCHUP

2 tablespoons olive oil
1 garlic clove, minced
1 small red onion, diced
One 14-ounce (400 g) can peeled plum tomatoes
1½ tablespoon tomato purée
1 tablespoon dark brown sugar
1 tablespoon red wine vinegar
Salt and pepper, to taste

1. Mix the tuna, onion, scallion, parsley, mayonnaise, and a few drops of tabasco in a bowl. Season with salt and pepper. Set aside.

2. **To prepare the ketchup:** Heat the olive oil in a saucepan over medium-high heat and sauté the garlic and onion until soft but not browned, about 2 to 3 minutes, stirring frequently. Add the peeled tomatoes, tomato purée, sugar, and vinegar. Cook over low heat until thickened, about 3 to 5 minutes. Season the ketchup with salt and pepper. Press the sauce through a fine sieve and leave to cool.

3. Butter each slice of bread on one side and turn over. Pile the tuna mixture onto the non-buttered sides of two slices of bread and top with the cheddar. Cover with the other two slices (buttered side up).

4. Bake the toasted sandwiches for 2 to 3 minutes on each side in a dry frying pan over medium heat until the bread is crunchy and the cheese has melted.

5. Cut the tuna melt diagonally and serve with the ketchup.

AVOCADO
TUNA SALAD

1 small red onion, sliced into thin rings
4 limes, juiced, plus zest of 1
½ avocado, cut into small cubes
2 tablespoons corn kernels
One 7-ounce (200 g) tin of albacore tuna
  in olive oil, drained
Extra virgin olive oil
Salt and pepper, to taste
½ bunch of cilantro, leaves only

1. Mix the red onion with the juice of 3 limes in a bowl and leave to infuse for a minimum of 20 minutes.

2. In another bowl, combine the avocado, and corn with the rest of the lime juice, the lime zest, and some olive oil. Season with salt and pepper. Stir in some of the pickled red onion and divide the salad between two plates. Carefully place a few chunks of albacore tuna on top of each portion and drizzle with olive oil. Garnish with the cilantro and serve.

TUNA AND OLIVE STUFFED ROMANO PEPPERS

>SERVES 2 AS A STARTER<

1 small red onion, diced
1 small garlic clove, minced
12 shiitake mushrooms, chopped
Half a 2-ounce (45 g) tin of
  anchovies, drained
One 5-ounce (140 g) tin of tuna in
  olive oil, drained
2 teaspoons capers
5 black olives, halved

2 romano peppers, halved
2 teaspoons panko (Japanese bread
  crumbs)
Zest of 1 lemon
¼ bunch of flat-leaf parsley, leaves
  only, finely chopped
Olive oil
Pepper

1. Preheat the oven to 350°F (180°C).

2. Heat a splash of olive oil over medium-high heat and sauté the red onion, garlic, and shiitake mushrooms until softened, 3 to 4 minutes. Add the anchovy fillets and let them "melt" in 2 minutes. Finally, mix in the tuna, capers, and olives and cook for a few more minutes until warmed through.

3. Meanwhile, brush the halved peppers with olive oil and place them in an ovenproof dish.

4. Remove the tuna mixture from the heat, fill the peppers with it, and dust with panko. Drizzle some extra olive oil on top and bake in the oven for 20 to 25 minutes, until crisp and done.

5. Scatter the lemon zest and the parsley over the peppers. Season with freshly ground black pepper and serve.

PITA WITH MAS HUNI
›SERVES 2 AS A LUNCH OR SNACK‹

In the Maldives—the Laamu Atoll, to be precise—where the skipjack tuna for this recipe is caught, the fishermen eat *mas huni* almost daily: a spicy tuna salad with coconut, lime, and fresh curry leaves. And when I say "spicy," I really mean it. This recipe calls for only one red chile, but the local islanders tend to use multiple and will happily serve this salad for breakfast.

1 small red onion, diced
1 red chile, seeded and finely
* chopped*
2 limes, juice of 1, wedges of 1
½ teaspoon salt
1 cup (90 g) freshly grated coconut★

½ bunch of cilantro (or 2 fresh
* curry leaves), finely chopped*
Two 6-ounce (160 g) tins of tuna in
* water, drained*
4 pieces of pita bread, sliced open
A few leaves of iceberg lettuce

1. Put on plastic gloves (or wrap sandwich bags around your hands) to protect your hands from the hot chiles. Work the red onion, chile, lime juice, and salt together in a bowl. In the Maldives, the ingredients are kneaded by hand to allow the flavors to blend.

2. Add the coconut, cilantro, and tuna and mix with a spoon until all the ingredients are combined and the tuna has a flaky texture. Set aside.

3. Prepare the pita breads according to the package directions or heat them to your liking using a toaster or toaster oven.

4. Fill the pitas with some lettuce and the mas huni and serve with the lime wedges.

★Note: If you prefer, you can use dried coconut flakes instead. Just add 2 tablespoons of coconut milk in addition to the flakes.

TUNA AND RICOTTA PASTA SALAD

›SERVES 2 AS A MAIN COURSE‹

Generous ½ cup (150 g) ricotta, strained

8 flat, square lasagna sheets, dried or fresh (if your noodles are rectangular, cut them in half to make squares)

¼ bunch of basil, leaves only, finely chopped

¼ bunch of tarragon, leaves only, finely chopped

Zest of 1 lemon

Salad mix of your choice, preferably including beet leaves

Two 5-ounce (140 g) tins of tuna in olive oil, drained

Extra virgin olive oil

Salt and pepper, to taste

1. **To strain the ricotta:** Take a strainer, line it with cheesecloth leaving some draping over the edge, and place it over a small bowl. Add the ricotta and then spread it into an even layer using a spatula or similar utensil. Cover the bowl with plastic wrap and chill in the refrigerator for at least 8 hours or overnight. Afterward, discard the liquid that's collected in the bowl.

2. **To make the pasta:** Once the ricotta is ready, cook the sheets of lasagna according to the package directions in plenty of salted water until al dente. Drain and briefly rinse under cold water until cool enough to handle.

3. Meanwhile, mix the drained ricotta with the basil and tarragon leaves, lemon zest, salt, and pepper. Set aside.

4. Construct the lasagna. Place a pasta sheet on each plate, scatter a few salad leaves on top, and then spoon on a dollop of the ricotta mixture, followed by some of the tuna. Repeat these layers until you've used up the lasagna and the other ingredients. End with tuna.

5. Drizzle with oil, season with black pepper, and serve.

TUNA BURGERS

►SERVES 2 AS A MAIN COURSE◄

*Two 6-ounce (160 g) tins of tuna
in water, drained*
*2 shallots, one finely diced, the other
thinly sliced into rings*
2 eggs, beaten
*6 tablespoons panko (Japanese
bread crumbs)*
*½ bunch of flat-leaf parsley, leaves
only*
Salt and pepper, to taste

4 tablespoons mayonnaise
Zest and juice of 1 lemon
1 avocado
*2 white buns (or any other kind of
burger bun)*
*1 scallion, white and light green
parts, thinly sliced into rings*
4 leaves of iceberg lettuce
Sunflower oil

1. Combine the tuna, shallot, eggs, panko, and parsley in a large bowl. Season with salt and pepper. Add some extra panko if the mixture is too wet. Shape the mixture into two burgers with your hands. Cover and chill in the fridge for 20 to 30 minutes to allow the burgers to firm up.

2. Mix the mayonnaise with the lemon zest and half of the juice in a bowl and set aside. Cut the avocado in half and remove the stone. Scoop out the flesh and cut into slices. Drizzle with the rest of the lemon juice to avoid discoloring and set aside.

3. Heat a grill pan over medium-high heat. Halve the buns and toast in the dry pan until they are a light golden brown. Set the buns aside, increase the heat, and take the tuna burgers out of the fridge. Brush with oil on both sides and place them in the grill pan. Carefully flip them over after 2 to 3 minutes, depending on thickness. Cook until they are golden brown on both sides and thoroughly heated through.

4. Assemble your burgers. Spread the buns with lemon mayonnaise. Place two lettuce leaves on the bottom of each bun. Top with a burger, followed by some slices of avocado, the scallion and shallot rings, and the other half of the bun. Serve immediately.

PASTA PUTTANESCA

‣SERVES 2 AS A MAIN COURSE‣

1 garlic clove, crushed
1 shallot, diced
4 anchovy fillets
One 14-ounce (400 g) can of
   peeled plum tomatoes
2 teaspoons red wine vinegar
2½ cups (200 g) penne (or any
   other kind of dried pasta)

10 Taggiasca olives, pitted
1 cup (100 g) halved cherry
   tomatoes
Two 5-ounce (140 g) tins of tuna in
   olive oil, drained
Salt and pepper
Olive oil
½ bunch of basil, leaves only

1. Heat a generous splash of olive oil in a frying pan over medium-high heat and cook the garlic and shallot for 2 to 3 minutes, until soft. Add the anchovy fillets and let them "melt" while stirring continuously, about 2 minutes.

2. Add the tomatoes and vinegar and let the mixture simmer for 3 to 4 minutes with a lid on, then crush with a potato masher.

3. Meanwhile, put a pan with plenty of salted water over medium-high heat and cook the penne according to the package directions.

4. Add the olives and cherry tomatoes to the shallot-tomato mixture and gently simmer for a few minutes over low heat. Fold in the drained tuna, heat through for 2 minutes, and season with pepper and salt if needed.

5. Once cooked, drain the penne in a colander and carefully stir the pasta through the tomato sauce. Divide the pasta puttanesca between two plates, drizzle with some olive oil, and serve garnished with basil.

TUNA SUMMER ROLLS

►SERVES 2 AS A LUNCH, SNACK, OR STARTER◄

Summer rolls are spring rolls that are eaten fresh rather than deep fried. Not only does this create a completely different taste sensation, but it makes them extra healthy, too!

ROLLS
¼ cucumber
½ carrot
½ avocado
Juice of ½ lemon
1 scallion
¾ cup (75 g) bean sprouts
Two 6-ounce (160 g) tins of tuna
  in water, drained
½ cup (50 g) roasted cashews,
  coarsely chopped

5 cups (100 g) loosely packed
  spinach
½ bunch of cilantro, leaves only
6 rice paper wrappers

DIP
3 tablespoons peanut butter
4 tablespoons soy sauce
2 tablespoons sesame oil
Juice of 1 lime

1. **To make the rolls:** Deseed the cucumber and cut into strips. Put them in a bowl and set aside. Cut the carrot into thin strips, put in a separate bowl, and also set aside. Scoop the avocado flesh out of its skin and slice into slivers. Put in a bowl with some lemon juice to stop them from discoloring and set aside. Trim the scallion and cut into matchsticks, put in a bowl, and set aside. Put the bean sprouts, tuna, cashews, spinach, and cilantro in separate bowls. Arrange all the ingredients in front of you.

2. Fill a large bowl with hot water and briefly soak one of the rice paper wrappers. Carefully spread it on a plate. Start by placing spinach leaves in the middle, and then top with a few strips of cucumber, carrot, and avocado before scattering on some scallion, bean sprouts, tuna, roasted cashews, and cilantro. Use only a little bit of each—pile on too much and the wrapper will tear. Carefully fold in the ends of the wrapper, then roll it up and cut in half. Repeat until all the rice paper wrappers are filled.

3. **To make the dip:** Stir together the peanut butter, soy sauce, sesame oil, and lime juice with a fork. Serve the summer rolls with the dip.

NIÇOISE SALAD
>SERVES 2 AS A LUNCH OR STARTER<

SALAD
½ cup (80 g) baby potatoes
⅓ cup (50 g) green beans, topped
   and tailed
2 eggs
2 heads of romaine lettuce, leaves
   detached and washed
10 black olives, halved
6 cherry tomatoes, halved
½ medium red onion, thinly sliced
   into rings

One 7-ounce (200 g) tin of
   albacore tuna in olive oil, drained
Half a 2-ounce (45 g) tin of
   anchovies, drained
Pepper, to taste

DRESSING
2 tablespoons sherry vinegar
2 teaspoons Dijon mustard
Pinch of salt
6 to 7 tablespoons olive oil

1. **To make the salad:** Put the baby potatoes in a medium pot with plenty of salted water and bring to a boil, then cook until fork-tender, about 10 to 15 minutes. Drain in a colander and briefly rinse under cold running water to cool a little. Do the same with the green beans, cooking until crisp-tender, about 2 to 4 minutes, then transfer to a bowl of cold water.

2. **To prepare the eggs:** Bring a saucepan of water to a boil and cook the eggs for 6 minutes, then run under cold water to chill for 2 minutes, peel, and set aside.

3. **To make the dressing:** Combine the vinegar, mustard, and salt in a bowl and beat with a fork. Add the olive oil in a trickle, beating continuously until the vinaigrette comes together. Halve the warm baby potatoes, place them in a bowl, and combine with some of the vinaigrette to let the flavors infuse. Leave to cool for a further 5 minutes before folding in the green beans.

4. Divide the lettuce between two deep plates and drizzle with some of the vinaigrette. Scatter the potatoes, green beans, olives, cherry tomatoes, and red onion on top. Top each portion with tuna and anchovy fillets. Serve with the eggs, halved, the rest of the vinaigrette, and pepper.

TUNA FRITTERS WITH TZATZIKI

►SERVES 2 AS A STARTER◄

FRITTERS
1 medium potato, peeled
½ zucchini
One 6-ounce (160 g) tin of tuna in
 water, drained
1 cup (150 g) canned corn, drained
½ bunch of parsley, leaves only,
 finely chopped
Heaping ⅓ cup (50 g) all-purpose
 flour
1 egg
2 teaspoons crushed chile flakes

Tabasco sauce
Salt and pepper, to taste
1 lemon, cut into wedges
Sunflower oil

TZATZIKI
½ cucumber, peeled
½ cup (125 g) full-fat Greek yogurt
Zest and juice of 1 lemon
1 small garlic clove, minced
Salt and pepper, to taste

1. **To make the fritters:** Coarsely grate the potato and zucchini and combine in a bowl. Add the tuna, corn, and parsley and mix thoroughly before adding the flour and the egg. Season with the chile flakes as well as tabasco, salt, and pepper. Set aside.

2. **To make the tzatziki:** Cut the cucumber in half lengthwise and deseed. Coarsely grate the flesh and put in a sieve. Using the rounded side of a spoon, press out as much liquid as possible and then combine the flesh in a bowl with the yogurt, lemon zest and juice, and garlic. Season with salt and pepper. Set aside.

3. Heat a generous splash of sunflower oil in a thick-bottomed frying pan over medium-high heat. Once the oil is hot enough, spoon two portions of the fritter mixture into the pan. Cook for 3 to 4 minutes until golden brown, flip the fritters, and bake for another 3 to 4 minutes, until crispy and done. Lift them out and drain on kitchen paper. Repeat until the mixture has been used up.

4. Serve the fritters alongside the lemon wedges, with the tzatziki in a separate bowl.

TUNA NOODLE SALAD WITH WAFU DRESSING

►SERVES 2 AS A MAIN COURSE◄

Wafu dressing is a traditional Japanese vinaigrette made with soy sauce, rice wine vinegar, mirin, and oil, which will often have sesame oil and/or sesame seeds added to it. In this dish it goes amazingly well with the noodles and tuna.

SALAD
1/4 cup (6 g) wakame
7 ounces (200 g) udon noodles
4 tablespoons sesame seeds
Two 6-ounce (160 g) tins of tuna in
   sunflower oil, drained
1 scallion, white and light green
   parts, thinly sliced into rings

WAFU DRESSING
2 tablespoons sesame oil
2 tablespoons canola oil
2 tablespoons rice wine vinegar
1 tablespoon mirin
1 tablespoon soy sauce

1. **To prepare the wakame:** Put the wakame in a bowl with 2 cups (1/2 L) of boiling water and leave to soak for 10 minutes. Drain the seaweed in a colander for 5 minutes, cut into 3/4-inch (2 cm) pieces, and leave to cool.

2. Cook the noodles according to the package directions.

3. Lightly toast the sesame seeds in a dry frying pan until golden. Set aside.

4. **To make the dressing:** Whisk the sesame oil, canola oil, rice wine vinegar, mirin, and soy sauce in a bowl. Set aside.

5. Drain the noodles in a colander, transfer to a bowl, and stir through the wakame and three quarters of the dressing. Divide the noodles between two bowls. Top each portion with tuna, sprinkle with the scallion and sesame seeds, and then drizzle with the rest of the dressing. Serve immediately.

THAI TUNA RED CURRY

1½ cups (150 g) rice, preferably long-grain

RED CURRY PASTE
1 small red onion, cut into chunks
1 stick of lemongrass, tough ends and outer leaves removed, cut into pieces
4 garlic cloves
¾-inch (2 cm) piece of ginger, peeled
3 Thai red chiles, stems removed
3 makrut lime leaves
½ bunch of cilantro
½ teaspoon turmeric
1 teaspoon tomato purée
Zest of 1 lime
¼ cup (50 ml) sunflower oil
Salt, to taste

CURRY
1 generous cup (250 ml) coconut milk
½ cup (50 g) canned bamboo shoots
1 cup (100 g) sugar snap peas, stringed (and blanched, optionally)
1 medium red bell pepper, cut into strips
Salt, to taste
Two 6-ounce (160 g) tins of tuna in sunflower oil, drained
Cilantro leaves, to taste
½ Thai red chile, seeded and cut into thin rings
1 lime, cut into wedges

1. Cook the rice according to the package directions. Set aside.

2. **To make the red curry paste:** Coarsely grind all the ingredients with some salt in a food processor. Set aside.

3. **To make the curry:** Heat 2 tablespoons of the red curry paste in a large wok and fry for 1 to 2 minutes until fragrant.

4. Add the coconut milk and stir until well mixed. Add the bamboo shoots, sugar snap peas, bell pepper, and salt and cook for 3 to 4 minutes, until tender. Carefully fold in the tuna and stir until everything is heated through.

5. Serve the tuna curry with the rice and garnish with cilantro, chile rings, and lime wedges.

Tip: Store any remaining curry paste in a sealed container in the fridge. It will keep for up to a week. Don't fancy making your own? Use a store-bought curry paste instead.

TUNA LASAGNA

1 garlic clove, halved
½ red chile, seeded and coarsely
  chopped
1 shallot, coarsely chopped
One 12-ounce (340 g) jar of roasted
  bell peppers, drained (or roast
  them yourself), cut into chunks
1 cup (250 g) tomato passata, from
  a can or a carton
½ bunch of basil, leaves only
1 small white onion, finely diced
2 vine-ripened tomatoes, seeded and
  diced
¼ bunch of oregano, leaves only
¼ bunch of thyme, leaves only

1 tablespoon red wine vinegar, plus
  extra if desired
⅓ cup (70 g) tomato purée
Two 5-ounce (140 g) tins of tuna in
  olive oil, drained
6 sheets of lasagna, uncooked
1 mozzarella ball, sliced
1 zucchini, spiralized or cut into
  long thin strips
1 eggplant, thinly sliced lengthwise
6 green asparagus spears
1⅓ cup (150 g) grated mild Gouda
Olive oil
Salt and pepper, to taste

1. Preheat the oven to 350°F (180°C).

2. Heat a splash of olive oil in a large frying pan over low heat and sauté the garlic, chile, and shallot for 2 to 3 minutes, until softened.

3. Add the roasted peppers and pour in the passata. Let the sauce simmer over low heat for 10 to 15 minutes. Add the basil and purée the mixture with an immersion blender until smooth. Set aside.

4. Heat a splash of olive oil over low heat and sauté the onion for 3 to 4 minutes, until softened. Add the diced tomato, oregano, thyme (hold back a few leaves), vinegar, and the roasted pepper sauce and simmer for 5 minutes. Season with salt and pepper. Stir in the tomato purée and the tuna, mix thoroughly, and leave on low heat for an additional 5 minutes. Add extra vinegar to taste.

5. Spread a layer of sauce in a baking dish (preferably 9 x 13 inches), followed by a layer of lasagna, and then some more of the sauce. Cover with half of the mozzarella, zucchini, and eggplant, then add another layer of sauce, lasagna, and sauce, and top with the rest of the mozzarella, vegetables, and finally the green asparagus. Top it off with a layer of sauce, lasagna, and sauce, and sprinkle with the Gouda and some freshly ground pepper.

6. Put the lasagna in the oven and bake for 45 minutes, until golden brown. To serve, scatter the remaining oregano and thyme leaves on top and drizzle with olive oil.

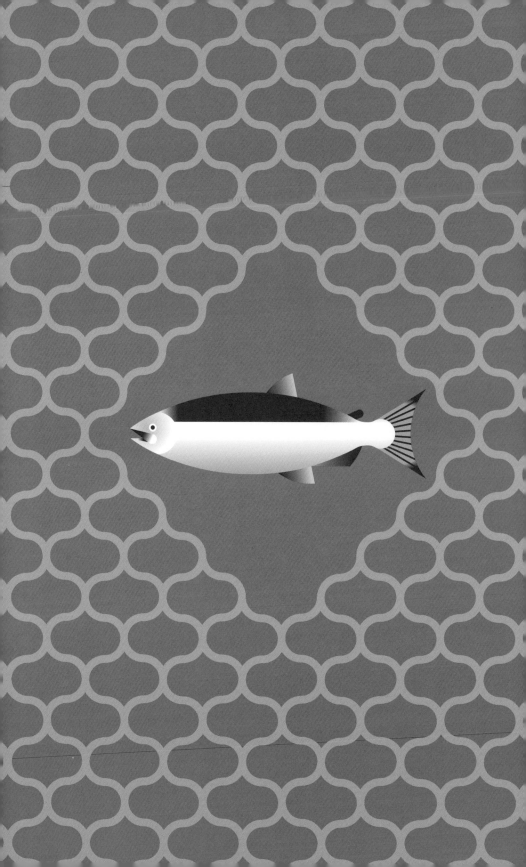

SALMON

SPECIES
Pink salmon (Oncorhynchus gorbuscha)

AVERAGE WEIGHT AND LENGTH
*6.6 pounds, 1 foot 3 inches long (3 kg and
40 cm)*

FISHING METHODS
Seine nets

MSC-CERTIFIED SALMON FISHERIES
*Southeast Alaska Purse Seining in Craig,
Alaska*
*Canadian Pacific Sustainable Fisheries Society
in Vancouver, Canada*
*Narody Severa Bolsheretsk in Kamchatka,
Russia*

SALMON

In recent years we've been eating more and more salmon—both fresh and frozen fillets, and the smoked variety. The rapid rise of salmon farming has especially boosted the popularity of this oily fish. Before the spread of farmed salmon, wild salmon was all we ate. The fish comes into this world at the source of a river and then migrates to the open sea, where it spends several years gorging itself before commencing the tough return journey upstream. There, at the top of the river, the salmon spawns to within four inches of its birthplace and then dies. Given its seasonality and the logistics of refrigeration, canning used to provide the ideal solution. The fish lends itself well to this process, as much of its nutritional value and omega-3 oils are retained: It allowed us to enjoy the rich flavor of salmon all year round.

When you buy a tin of salmon, chances are that the fish was caught in Alaska. That's good to know, not least because it means that you can eat with a clear conscience. Salmon stocks in Alaska have been traditionally well-managed. The same is true for the salmon populations off the west coast of Canada. Because a lot of the deep-red sockeye salmon is sold fresh and frozen, you'll find proportionally more pink salmon in cans on supermarket shelves (the color may be a little paler, but it's no less tasty), though you may also come across tinned sockeye. For the following salmon recipes, either will do! Canned salmon is also available skinless and boneless for easy use, or *with* skin and bones. But fear not: Conservation softens the bones, which can actually add a bit of nice, nutritious bite—for those who like that kind of thing.

For the salmon in the distinctive tapered cans we need to travel to Craig—a village in the west of the state, overlooking the Gulf of Alaska. It's pink salmon they fish around here. In the summer, the fishermen set off in small vessels with seine nets, in search of well-fed, oily salmon at the mouth of the river. While moving through the water the fishermen draw a net around a school, which is then pulled closed at the bottom, trapping the salmon in a kind of basket. The tasty, natural product that the local fishing community then lands in small numbers is processed into skinless and boneless canned salmon.

RED, REDDER, REDDEST

Most of the salmon consumed in the US is farmed or fished from Alaskan waters and includes the chinook, chum, coho, pink, and sockeye varieties. The wild salmon are born at the source of a river and swim downstream to the sea. All are anadromous fish, which means that after spending several years hunting at sea they will migrate back to their natal stream, swimming against the strong current to spawn at the top. This could be within 4 inches of where the fish originally hatched. The salmon's food determines the eventual color of its flesh. Having fed on small shrimp and lobster, sockeye is dark red, chum is a little lighter, and the color of pink salmon . . . you've guessed it. Of these, pink salmon is the variety most commonly canned.

TINNED SALMON 2.0

Salmon's pink flesh is famed for its fabulous flavor and its high levels of omega-3 fatty acids and vitamin D. For these reasons, tinned salmon has evolved into a widely consumed staple. Tinned salmon used to have a poor reputation, and those of an older generation may remember the once-ubiquitous cans of low-quality fish complete with skin and bones. But over the years the quality of tinned salmon has vastly improved, so its current popularity is well deserved. Tinned salmon is back! And let's not forget that it lends itself to delicious cooking. The local fishermen in Alaska prefer their pink salmon fresh, dried, or from a wood-fired grill, but I'd like to introduce you to even more innovative creations you can make with the canned variety. Served on a delicious pizza, for example (p. 66) or with scrambled eggs and toast (p. 58).

KNOWLEDGE IS POWER

Fish stocks in Alaska are strictly monitored by the Alaska Department of Fish and Game. As early as 1959, shortly after the territory was proclaimed a US state, a law was passed to protect the salmon population. And to this day the government continues to invest greatly in equipment that measures salmon stocks in the rivers. Thanks to the state's sustainable management, all salmon caught in Alaska is MSC-certified.

SALMON SCRAMBLED EGGS ON TOAST

›SERVES 2 AS A BREAKFAST OR BRUNCH‹

2 slices of bread
6 eggs
2 tablespoons milk
1 tablespoon (15 g) butter
One 6-ounce (170 g) tin of salmon, drained
½ bunch of chives, finely chopped
½ scallion, white and light green parts,
*   sliced into thin rings*
Scant 2 tablespoons salmon roe (optional)
Salt and pepper, to taste

1. Toast the slices of bread in a toaster or toaster oven.

2. Beat the eggs and milk with a fork in a bowl and season with salt and pepper.

3. Melt the butter in a frying pan over low heat. Pour the beaten egg mixture into the pan and stir with a wooden spoon. Pause every 10 seconds for 10 seconds, allowing the egg to gradually set. Add the salmon and half of the chives and scallion when the eggs are nearly set, and warm through for 1 minute.

4. Divide the scrambled eggs between the slices of bread, top with the salmon roe, if using, and the rest of the chives and scallion. Season with freshly ground pepper and serve.

SALMON AND SPINACH SALAD WITH COCONUT DRESSING

>SERVES 2 AS A LUNCH OR APPETIZER<

SALAD

½ cup (100 g) quinoa
4 tablespoons sesame seeds
3 tablespoons cashews, coarsely
  chopped
8 cups (200 g) fresh spinach
1 cup (50 g) chopped thin
  asparagus
½ shallot, finely chopped
One 6-ounce (170 g) tin of salmon,
  drained

3 tablespoons freshly grated
  coconut*
Seeds of ½ pomegranate
½ bunch of cilantro, leaves only
Salt and pepper, to taste

DRESSING

¼ cup (50 ml) coconut milk
Zest and juice of 2 limes
2 tablespoons sesame oil, plus extra
⅓-inch (1 cm) piece of ginger,
  peeled and minced

1. Cook the quinoa according to the package directions. Set aside and leave to cool.

2. **To make the dressing:** Combine the coconut milk, lime juice and zest, sesame oil, and ginger in a small bowl. Set aside.

3. **To make the salad:** Briefly toast the sesame seeds and the cashews in a dry frying pan until lightly colored. Leave to cool.

4. Put the spinach and the asparagus in a large salad bowl, stir in the shallot and the salmon, add the quinoa, and pour the dressing over it. Mix everything thoroughly and season with salt and pepper.

5. Sprinkle the sesame seeds, cashews, coconut, and pomegranate seeds on top. Serve the salad garnished with the cilantro leaves and, if desired, extra sesame oil.

*Note: If you prefer, you can use dried coconut flakes instead. Just add 2 tablespoons of coconut milk in addition to the flakes.

SALMON CAKES
WITH CHIMICHURRI

>SERVES 2 AS AN APPETIZER OR SNACK<

SALMON CAKES

½ pound (250 g) floury potatoes,
   peeled and halved
2 scallions, white and light green
   parts, thinly sliced
Handful of arugula, coarsely chopped
½ bunch of chives, finely chopped
1 teaspoon cayenne pepper
Salt and pepper, to taste
1 egg, beaten
One 6-ounce (170 g) tin of salmon,
   drained
Sunflower oil, for frying
Flour, for dusting
½ lime

AVOCADO SPREAD

1 avocado, stoned and flesh removed
½ shallot, finely diced
Juice of 1 lemon
1 tablespoon olive oil
Salt and pepper, to taste

CHIMICHURRI

½ red chile, seeded
1 garlic clove
2 teaspoons dried oregano
1 shallot, halved
¼-inch (3 cm) piece of ginger,
   peeled and coarsely chopped
1 bunch of mint, leaves only
1 bunch of cilantro
Juice of 2 lemons
2 tablespoons red wine vinegar
2 tablespoons olive oil

1. **To make the salmon cakes:** Boil the potatoes in plenty of salted water until done, approximately 15 minutes. Drain and leave to cool. Roughly mash them before mixing in the scallion, arugula, chives, and cayenne pepper. Season with salt and pepper. Lastly, add the egg and the salmon, and mash with a fork until everything comes together in a coarse mixture.

2. Shape the potato-salmon mixture into balls that fit in the palm of your hand, then flatten them until they are between ½ and ¾ inch thick. Leave the cakes to firm up in the fridge for 30 minutes.

3. **To make the spread:** Mash the avocado with the shallot, lemon juice, and some olive oil, and season with salt and pepper. Set the spread aside.

4. **To make the chimichurri:** Purée all the ingredients in a food processor until smooth. Add extra olive oil if the sauce is too thick. Set aside.

5. Heat a splash of sunflower oil in a thick-bottomed frying pan over medium heat. Dust the salmon cakes with a bit of flour and fry them for 3 minutes, until golden brown. Carefully flip them over with a spatula and fry on the other side for 3 more minutes. The cakes should be nice and hot inside. Lift them out of the pan with a slotted turner and onto paper towels. (You can also keep them warm in the oven until all portions are cooked, if you prefer.) Serve the salmon cakes with the avocado spread, chimichurri, and lime.

SALMON CANNELLONI

>SERVES 2 AS A MAIN COURSE<

¾ cup (200 g) ricotta, strained
⅓ cup (50 g) green peas, fresh or
   frozen
Two 6-ounce (170 g) tins of
   salmon, drained
Zest of 1 lemon
Salt and pepper, to taste

2½ tablespoons (40 g) butter
⅓ cup (40 g) all-purpose flour
1⅛ cup (250 ml) milk
1⅛ cup (250 ml) fish stock
6 cannelloni shells
½ cup (50 g) grated Parmesan

1. **To strain the ricotta:** Take a strainer, line it with cheesecloth leaving some draping over the edge, and place it over a small bowl. Add the ricotta and then spread it into an even layer using a spatula or similar utensil. Cover the bowl with plastic wrap and chill in the refrigerator for at least 8 hours or overnight. Afterward, discard the liquid that's collected in the bowl.

2. Heat a pan of water over high heat, and, as soon as it comes to a boil, blanch the peas for 2 minutes. Drain and leave to cool a little.

3. Mix the salmon with the ricotta and the lemon zest, carefully stir through the peas, and season with salt and pepper. Set aside.

4. Preheat the oven to 350°F (180°C).

5. Melt the butter in a saucepan over low heat. Add the flour and stir with a whisk until the mixture thickens. Cook for around 30 seconds, and then slowly, bit by bit, pour in the milk and the stock, stirring all the while until the sauce is smooth and thick, about 3 to 4 minutes. Season with salt and pepper and set aside.

6. Spoon the ricotta mixture into a piping bag and fill the cannelloni shells. (Alternatively, use a sandwich bag with one of its corners cut off.) Pour some of the white sauce into a rectangular baking pan, put in the tubes, and pour the rest of the sauce on top. Sprinkle with grated cheese and a grinding of black pepper.

7. Place the cannelloni in the oven and bake for 45 minutes, until golden brown. Serve straight from the oven.

SALMON PIZZA

►SERVES 2 AS A SNACK OR MAIN COURSE◄

PIZZA
2 cups (250 g) flour
1 level teaspoon salt
½ cup (120 ml) tepid water
1 tablespoon olive oil, plus extra
1 tablespoon plus 1 teaspoon (15 g)
   active dry yeast
Two 6-ounce (170 g) tins of
   salmon, drained
1 mozzarella ball, sliced
½ cup (50 g) shaved Parmesan

½ bunch of basil, leaves only,
   roughly torn
Salt and pepper, to taste

PESTO
1 bunch of basil, leaves only
2 garlic cloves, peeled
½ cup (50 g) Parmesan
¼ cup (30 g) pine nuts
½ cup (100 ml) olive oil
Salt and pepper, to taste

1. **To make the pizza dough:** Sift the flour on the kitchen counter and mix in the salt. Shape into a mound with your hands and form a well inside. Pour the tepid water and the olive oil into a separate bowl. Add the yeast and stir until it's fully dissolved. Pour the yeast mixture into the well of the flour.

2. Work the flour and yeast mixture together. Knead the dough for about 10 minutes until smooth and elastic. The longer you knead, the better. Shape the dough into a ball and leave in a bowl, covered with a damp tea towel, to rise for 3 hours at room temperature. The volume should nearly double.

3. Preheat the oven to 425°F (220°C).

4. Place the dough on a floured work surface. Gently knock the air out of it with your hands and then roll it out with a rolling pin into a large pizza crust about ¼ inch (5 mm) thick. Coat a baking sheet with oil or line it with parchment paper. Place the dough on it and push it to the sides so the entire sheet is covered. Set aside.

5. **To make the pesto:** Put the basil leaves, garlic, Parmesan, and pine nuts in a food processor. Coarsely grind before adding the olive oil in a slow trickle until it reaches the desired consistency. Season with salt and pepper.

6. Spread a generous amount of pesto on the pizza base. Top with the salmon, mozzarella, and Parmesan. Slide the baking sheet into the oven and bake the pizza for 10 to 12 minutes, until crispy and done. Garnish with basil leaves and extra virgin olive oil and serve.

Tip: Instead of making your own pizza base, you can buy one ready to bake.

ANCHOVIES

SPECIES
European anchovy (Engraulis encrasicolus)
Argentine anchovy (Engraulis anchoita)

MAXIMUM WEIGHT AND LENGTH
European anchovy: 1 ounce, 7.9 inches long
*   (30 g and 20 cm)*
Argentine anchovy: .88 ounce, 6.7 inches long
*   (25 g and 17 cm)*

FISHING METHODS
Seine nets, pelagic trawls

MSC-CERTIFIED ANCHOVY FISHERIES
Cantabrian Sea Fishery in Cantabria, Spain
*   (European anchovy)*
Argentine Anchovy Fishery (Bonaerense stock) in
*   Mar del Plata, Argentina (Argentine anchovy)*

SMALL IS BEAUTIFUL

The seaside town of Mar del Plata is located some 250 miles (400 km) south of Argentina's capital, Buenos Aires. Look beyond the beaches dotted with colorful umbrellas, and leave the boulevard thronged with tourists behind, and you'll arrive at a small port. Moored at the jetties are the bright orange boats belonging to the local fishing community. For a long time, the waters around here were overfished. Bad news for the environment and the anchovy's survival, as well as for the fishermen who depend on the fish for their livelihood. That's why, around ten years ago, the local community changed tack. Rules were drawn up and innovations implemented. In 2011, the anchovy fishery in Mar del Plata became the first in the world to earn an MSC certification.

As the coast disappears from view, the fishermen start their search for the anchovies. Once they localize a shoal, they circle it with a net. Then the bottom is pulled closed and the net hauled on board so they can check the size of the anchovies. If the fish are too small, the net is opened up again and they have another go. In this way, the fishermen ensure that the young anchovies stay alive to mature and reproduce.

Afterward, the anchovies are brought onshore, where their heads and guts are removed right away. Next, the anchovies are salt-cured and stored in barrels. They spend six to seven months there, ripening at a carefully monitored temperature. Then the barrels are transferred to Mutriku, a small town in the north of Spain. Here we find the Yurrita cannery, a family-owned business founded in 1867 by José Miguel Mauleón. The original canning factory began life in the cellar of the Yurrita family home. Today the fifth generation is at the helm, and the company focuses on curing and processing anchovy, tuna, crab, and squid.

There are three fundamental factors that determine the taste of anchovy, as an older member of the Mauleón family explains. First off: a lengthy ripening process at the right temperature. After that, the salted anchovy must be rinsed thoroughly to arrive at the desired salt content. Finally, the fish must be carefully filleted to remove every last trace of bone. The latter two steps are taken care of at Yurrita. As is the canning, which is done with top-quality oil, and which brings us full circle—from sustainably caught fish to mouthwatering tin.

THE ANCHOVY FAMILY TREE

The anchovy has earned itself a place in kitchens the world over because the little fish is found virtually everywhere. There are no fewer than 139 species! Two of the best-known varieties are the European and Argentine anchovy. The small, herring-like fish live in temperate, open seas, feed on plankton and algae, and swim in large shoals. The European anchovy is native to the northeastern Atlantic Ocean, its Argentine sibling to the southwestern Atlantic.

POWERHOUSE

It may be small in stature, but the anchovy packs a punch: We tend to see it as a rich flavoring ingredient from a can. And while we may snack on the odd fillet while cooking, we know that the salty fish is best used in small doses. In many southern European coastal regions, anchovy fillets are melted in hot oil as a basis for all kinds of dishes. This imparts a unique flavor, and often it won't be necessary to add extra salt later. The oily fish lifts simple dishes such as a potato gratin (p. 82) and an endive salad (p. 77) to a higher level. And while it may be salty, don't be afraid to give the anchovy more of a starring role. Why not serve it whole on bread with tomato confit (p. 74)? Often it's the little things that make the difference!

RAPID REPRODUCTION

MSC-certified anchovy fisheries can be found in a Spanish town on the coast of Cantabria and in Mar del Plata in Argentina. The latter was the first to be certified, in 2011, while its counterpart in Spain—situated on the Bay of Biscay—followed in 2015. In 2001, anchovy stocks in the Bay of Biscay plummeted, leading to the five-year closure of the fishery. But anchovies reproduce fast, so stocks have now been restored to their former state. Today, the fish population is well managed and carefully monitored, while the fishermen stick to a long-term plan to keep stocks healthy.

ANCHOVIES WITH TOMATO CONFIT ON TOAST

›SERVES 2 AS AN APPETIZER OR SNACK‹

Extra virgin olive oil
20 cherry tomatoes
2 garlic cloves, peeled and halved
¼ bunch of thyme
Salt and pepper, to taste
½ loaf of ciabatta (or your favorite bread)
One 2-ounce (45 g) tin of anchovies in olive oil,
  drained
½ bunch of basil, leaves only, shredded

1. Preheat the oven to 350°F (180°C).

2. Heat a splash of olive oil in a frying pan over medium-high heat. Cut the cherry tomatoes in half and place them in the oil with their cut side down. Turn down the heat, add the garlic and thyme, and, with the lid on, leave the tomatoes to soften for 10 to 15 minutes. Season with salt and pepper.

3. Slice the ciabatta and toast the bread in a toaster or toaster oven.

4. Top the warm bread with the confit tomatoes and discard the garlic and thyme. Divide the anchovy fillets between the slices, sprinkle with the basil leaves, and drizzle with olive oil to taste.

ANCHOVY AND ENDIVE SALAD

►SERVES 2 AS A LUNCH OR APPETIZER◄

SALAD

2 heads of Belgian endive
½ Granny Smith apple, cored and
  diced
Handful of walnuts, coarsely
  chopped
2 celery stalks
½ cup (60 g) shaved Manchego
  cheese
Half a 2-ounce (45 g) tin of
  anchovies in olive oil, drained

DRESSING

2 tablespoons mayonnaise
Zest and juice of ½ lemon
A few sprigs of flat-leaf parsley,
  leaves only, finely chopped, plus
  extra
Salt and pepper, to taste

1. **To make the salad:** Strip the endive of its outer leaves, discarding the bitter core, and rinse them under cold water. Combine the leaves with the diced apple and pieces of walnut. Set aside.

2. Break the celery stalks in half and thinly slice the stalks. Add them to the endive mix.

3. **To make the dressing:** Whisk the mayonnaise with the lemon zest, juice, and parsley in a small bowl. Season with salt and pepper.

4. Combine the endive salad with the dressing and divide between two plates. Sprinkle with the Manchego cheese and top each portion with a few anchovy fillets. Garnish with some extra parsley and serve.

ANCHOVY DUMPLINGS

►SERVES 2 AS AN APPETIZER OR SNACK◄

1¼ cup (150 g) flour
½ cup (100 ml) boiling water
Sesame oil
Corn starch, for dusting
¾ cup (50 g) shiitake mushrooms,
   finely chopped
1½ cup (100 g) bok choy, finely
   shredded
¼ cup (25 g) carrots, cut into matchsticks
Half a 2-ounce (45 g) tin of anchovies in
   olive oil, drained, very finely chopped

3 scallions, white and light green
   parts, minced
⅓-inch (1 cm) piece of ginger, peeled and
   minced
½ cup (125 ml) soy sauce
1 teaspoon Shaoxing rice wine
1 egg
Salt and pepper, to taste
3 tablespoons sesame seeds
Sunflower oil, for frying
⅛ red chile, seeded and sliced into rings

1. **To make the dumplings:** Add the flour to a bowl, gradually pour in the hot water, and stir with a fork until you have a coherent dough. Dust a work surface with cornstarch and knead the dough for about 10 minutes until elastic. Add more water if it's too dry or extra flour if it's too wet. Shape the dough into a long cylinder, wrap it in plastic, and let it rest at room temperature for 30 minutes.

2. Meanwhile, prepare the filling. Heat some sesame oil in a frying pan over medium-high heat and sauté the mushrooms, bok choy, carrots, anchovies, scallions (reserving a little for garnish), and ginger for about 4 minutes, until softened. Leave to cool completely and then drain thoroughly. Mix in 1 tablespoon of soy sauce, the rice wine, and the egg, and season with salt and pepper. Store in the fridge until you're ready to serve.

3. Bring a large pan of water to a boil. Meanwhile, cut the dough cylinder on a work surface dusted with cornstarch into small pieces of about ½ ounce (14 g) each and shape them into balls. Cover with plastic wrap and use a rolling pin to flatten each ball into a round wrapper about 3 inches (8 cm) in diameter.

4. Place a wrapper in the palm of your hand and place 1 teaspoon of filling in the middle. Moisten the edge of the dough with water, fold the wrapper into a half moon, and firmly press down the edges into small pleats. Repeat until all the wrappers have been filled. Line a steaming basket with parchment paper, put in the dumplings, and steam them over the pan of boiling water for 15 minutes, until done.

5. Meanwhile, toast the sesame seeds in a dry frying pan until golden brown and let them cool. Then heat some sunflower oil in a large frying pan over medium-high heat and fry the dumplings for 2 minutes on each side until golden brown.

6. **To make the dip:** Combine the rest of the soy sauce with most of the toasted sesame seeds and the chile.

7. Arrange the dumplings on a plate, sprinkle the rest of the scallion and the sesame seeds on top, and serve with the dip.

ARTICHOKE WITH ANCHOVY DIP

►SERVES 2 AS AN APPETIZER OR SNACK◄

1 lemon, halved
2 tablespoons flour
2 large artichokes
Half a 2-ounce (45 g) tin of
   anchovies in olive oil, drained

Scant ½ cup (100 ml) olive oil
3 tablespoons white wine vinegar
3 teaspoons Dijon mustard
Pepper, to taste

1. Bring a large pan of water—big enough to hold the artichokes—to a boil with the lemon halves and the flour. Twist (don't cut!) the stems off the artichokes, pulling away as many of the tough fibers as you can.

2. Put the artichokes in the boiling water and place a deep soup plate (or smaller pot lid) on top of them so they remain upright and under water. Cook the artichokes for about 45 minutes, until the bottom leaves come off easily.

3. Meanwhile, combine the anchovies, olive oil, white wine vinegar, mustard, and some pepper in a food processor. Add 1 to 2 tablespoons of the artichoke cooking water to taste.

4. Scoop the artichokes out of the water with a slotted spoon and put them on a platter. Serve with the dip.

Note: Adding lemon and flour to the cooking water lets the artichokes retain their pretty light-green color.

FISHY POTATO
AU GRATIN DAUPHINOISE

›SERVES 2 AS A MAIN COURSE‹

1 garlic clove, halved
1 tablespoon (15 g) butter
One 2-ounce (45 g) tin of
*   anchovies in olive oil, drained*
⅜ cup (40 g) grated Gruyère
½ cup (100 ml) heavy cream
1 egg, beaten

¼ bunch thyme, leaves only, finely
*   chopped, plus extra*
¼ bunch oregano, leaves only, finely
*   chopped*
1 pound (400 g) russet potatoes,
*   peeled*
Salt and pepper, to taste

1. Preheat the oven to 350°F (175°C).

2. Rub a baking dish with the garlic and then grease with the butter. Set aside.

3. Whisk together the anchovies, half of the Gruyère, heavy cream, egg, thyme, and oregano. Slice the potatoes and add to the cream mixture until they're all evenly coated. Arrange the potato slices in the greased baking dish, overlapping slightly, and cover with any remaining cream left in the bowl. Sprinkle with the rest of the Gruyère.

4. Bake the potato gratin for approximately 50 minutes, until golden brown. Garnish with extra thyme leaves and serve immediately.

CAULIFLOWER STEAK WITH MUSHROOMS AND ANCHOVY BUTTER

►SERVES 2 AS A MAIN COURSE◄

One 2-ounce (45 g) tin of
  anchovies in olive oil, drained
¾ cup (200 g) butter (at room
  temperature), plus extra
½ pound (200 g) French fingerling
  potatoes, halved
Olive oil
2 garlic cloves, one crushed and one
  halved
Salt and pepper, to taste

½ bunch of rosemary
1 large cauliflower
1 teaspoon nutmeg
1½ cups (150 g) mixed mushrooms
  (such as oyster, beech, and
  chestnut mushrooms), chopped
  into pieces
½ cup (50 g) roasted pecans,
  coarsely chopped

1. Preheat the oven to 350°F (180°C).

2. Combine the anchovy fillets with the butter in a food processor until it forms a thick mass. Scoop the mixture onto plastic wrap and roll it into a neat, thick tube. Let it set in the fridge.

3. Spread the potatoes on a baking sheet lined with parchment paper, drizzle with olive oil, and rub in the crushed garlic with your hands. Season with salt and pepper and scatter the sprigs of rosemary on top. Roast the potatoes for 30 to 35 minutes, until golden brown.

4. Meanwhile, cut two large, flat "steaks" from the middle of the cauliflower. Rub both sides with the garlic halves and sprinkle with nutmeg, salt, and pepper.

5. Melt the extra butter in a frying pan over medium-high heat and cook the cauliflower steaks, flipping them regularly, for a total of 5 minutes on each side. Add the mushrooms halfway through the cooking time.

6. Take the anchovy butter out of the fridge and cut into slices. Serve each cauliflower steak with a slice of anchovy butter, along with the roasted potatoes, sautéed mushrooms, and pecans.

Tip: The remaining anchovy butter will keep in the fridge for 2 to 3 days. It's great on toast or on a baguette!

SARDINES

SPECIES
European sardine (Sardina pilchardus)

MAXIMUM WEIGHT AND LENGTH
2.3 ounces, 9.8 inches long (65 g and 25 cm)

FISHING METHODS
Ring nets

MSC-CERTIFIED SARDINE FISHERIES
*Cornish Sardine Fishery in Newlyn Harbour,
   Cornwall, United Kingdom*
*Association des Bolincheurs de Bretagne, Bay of
   Biscay, France*

ENGLISH WIT

The sardine fishers who set sail from Newlyn Harbour do so in a total of fourteen small vessels equipped with ring nets, three or four fishermen to a boat. During the brief season, the setting sun marks the start of their search for the finest, oiliest sardines in English waters: the anchors are raised, the bright yellow buoys attached to the boats are pulled up, and schools of sardines are localized shortly before the fleet sets off.

The sardines, which swim in large schools and are lured to the surface with bright lights, are encircled by a net that's closed off at the bottom. In the dead of night this heavy net full of fish is winched up. Then, with a scoop net, the sardines are transferred to the hold so they keep fresh until the boat comes ashore again in Cornwall not long after.

The sardines are taken straight from the boat to a specialist processor—A Poveira in Portugal—which has been canning fish since 1938. As soon as the sardines arrive here, they're placed in a saltwater bath. Next up, the fish are cleaned, their heads and guts removed, and then rinsed again. Then the fillets are steamed at 212°F (100°C). This is a unique method, since many factories don't cook the sardines until they're in the tin. Afterward, the sardines are left to dry to remove all traces of water. Following this, the fish are checked manually, cut to size, and put into tins. Finally, the tins are filled with oil, sauce, or other flavorings and sealed. Then they go straight through to the final phase, in which they're sterilized for 60 minutes at 212°F (100°C). This gives the tinned sardines a shelf life of no fewer than five years, and means we can enjoy the very best fish all year round.

CORNISH SARDINES

Sardines swim all over the world, but only in subtropical climates. The European sardine—the *Sardina pilchardus*—can be found from Portugal and Brittany up to Cornwall. In Cornwall the English are adamant that there's only one proper sardine: the Cornish sardine, also known as the pilchard. The English don't like to admit it, but these are in fact the same fish as those caught by the southern Europeans, except in a different region and at a later point in the season. By the time the sardine reaches Cornwall, the fish is fully grown and really oily. Just how the English like them. As do we!

LIKE A GOOD WINE

Many European coastal regions have their own tradition of tinned sardines. Sardines have been tinned for almost two hundred years. In the nineteenth century, the fish were considered to be a real delicacy by the upper classes. They're caught in all shapes and sizes, and their distinctive taste makes them a good match for the various sauces and other flavorings that are added in different cultures. On the south coast of Brittany, the French stubbornly claim that the small, oily fish was first canned in their part of the world. This stretch of coastline still boasts many factories where *sardines au beurre*—sardines with butter—roll off the production line.

Connoisseurs in Spain and Portugal swear by sardines in oil. The plainer, the better. They then let these tins mature, like a bottle of good wine, in a dark cellar. The tins are frequently turned over to prevent the fillets from drying out on one side. Significantly, the fillets inside are whole, complete with skin and bones. After maturing, the sardines are traditionally served with toast and a glass of chilled white wine.

Those who prefer to cook with the fillets should opt for sardines in water for cold dishes and sardines in oil for warm ones. So if you're making quinoa tabbouleh (p. 95), you should use sardines in water, but if you're preparing the leek tart with tarragon (p. 99), you need sardines in olive or sunflower oil. Sardines with an added flavor, like tomato sauce or olive oil with lemon, are best eaten on their own with some good bread.

CAN YOU HAVE TOO MUCH OF A GOOD THING?

Dozens of years ago, many sardine fisheries were overexploiting stocks; in other words, they were fishing too much. But a new dawn has broken, one in which much better care is taken of fish populations, so they've been restored to health. Not only do the fishermen now stick to their quotas, but they also use methods that avoid bycatch and damage to the environment. The sardine fishery in Cornwall has been MSC-certified since 2010.

SARDINE HUMMUS

›SERVES 2 AS AN APPETIZER OR SNACK‹

Half a 14-ounce (400 g) can of
  chickpeas, drained
½ garlic clove
2 tablespoons tahini
Juice of ½ lemon
½ bunch of flat-leaf parsley, tough
  stalks removed, plus extra leaves
1 tablespoon crushed chile flakes
1 teaspoon tabasco

1 teaspoon ground cumin
1 teaspoon salt
3 tablespoons water, plus extra (optional)
3 tablespoons extra virgin olive oil,
  plus extra (optional)
Half a 4.2-ounce (120 g) tin of
  sardines in olive oil, drained
1 teaspoon hot smoked paprika
Salt and pepper, to taste

1. Coarsely grind the chickpeas, garlic, tahini, lemon juice, parsley, chile flakes, tabasco, cumin, and salt in a food processor. Slowly pour in the water and the olive oil and process until smooth. Add extra water and/or olive oil for a creamier texture. Season with salt and pepper.

2. Put the hummus in a bowl and top with the sardines. Scatter the extra parsley and the paprika on top and drizzle with olive oil.

FAVA WITH ANCHOVIES

›SERVES 2 AS AN APPETIZER OR SNACK‹

Extra virgin olive oil
1 small yellow onion, diced
1¼ cup (250 g) yellow split peas, rinsed
1 bay leaf
Juice of ½ lemon, plus extra (optional)

Salt and pepper, to taste
Half a 2-ounce (45 g) tin of
  anchovies in olive oil, drained
1 teaspoon za'atar

1. Heat some olive oil in a thick-bottomed frying pan over low heat and soften the onion for 3 to 4 minutes, until translucent. Add the split peas and briefly sauté with the onion. Add the bay leaf and enough water to cover the peas by a ½ inch (1 cm). Bring to a boil, turn down the heat, and cook the peas with the lid loosely on for 30 to 40 minutes, until soft. Add water if it looks like the peas might be boiling dry.

2. Take the pan off the heat when the peas are soft and creamy, remove the bay leaf, and put the lid back on. Let rest for 30 minutes.

3. Grind the peas with the lemon juice, 2 to 3 splashes of extra virgin olive oil, and salt and pepper in a food processor until smooth. Add extra olive oil and/or lemon juice to taste.

4. Serve the pea purée with the anchovies, za'atar, and extra olive oil.

QUINOA TABBOULEH WITH SARDINES

Heaping ⅓ cup (60 g) quinoa
2 bunches parsley, finely chopped
¼ bunch mint, leaves only, finely chopped
1 scallion, finely chopped
½ jalapeño, finely chopped
2 cups (200 g) cherry tomatoes, seeded and diced,
  with a few tomatoes quartered
Zest and juice of 2 lemons
Salt and pepper, to taste
Extra virgin olive oil
Two 4.2-ounce (120 g) tins of sardines in olive oil,
  drained

1. Cook the quinoa according to the package directions. Set aside and leave to cool.

2. Put the parsley, mint, scallion, jalapeño, and diced tomato into a large bowl and stir in the cooked quinoa. Add the lemon zest and juice, season with salt and pepper, and make the tabbouleh extra creamy with a generous splash of olive oil.

3. Top the tabbouleh with the sardine fillets and the quartered tomatoes and serve.

SARDINE EGGPLANT BRAIDS

►SERVES 2 AS AN APPETIZER OR SNACK◄

2 eggplants
Olive oil
Salt and pepper, to taste
One 4.2-ounce (120 g) tin of
    sardines in olive oil, drained
2 tablespoons shelled pistachios,
    coarsely chopped

2 tablespoons hazelnuts, coarsely
    chopped
¼ bunch mint, leaves only
Seeds from ½ pomegranate
Juice of ½ lemon

1. Preheat the oven to 425°F (220°C).

2. Thinly slice the eggplants lengthwise and discard the tops. Arrange the slices on a baking sheet lined with parchment paper, drizzle with olive oil, and season with salt and pepper. Roast the eggplant in the oven for 15 minutes until golden brown. Warm the sardines on a separate tray during the final 3 minutes.

3. Meanwhile, heat a frying pan over medium-high heat and dry-roast the pistachios and hazelnuts until lightly colored, about 4 to 6 minutes. Set aside.

4. Divide the eggplant slices between two plates, interlacing them on each plate. Top the eggplant with the sardines, sprinkle with the pistachios and hazelnuts, mint leaves, pomegranate seeds, and salt and pepper. Drizzle with lemon juice and olive oil. Serve immediately.

SARDINE AND LEEK TART WITH TARRAGON

►SERVES 2 TO 4 AS A MAIN COURSE◄

Olive oil
2 garlic cloves, minced
1 small yellow onion, thinly sliced into rings
2 small leeks, washed and sliced into rings
2 eggs
Salt and pepper, to taste

1 tablespoon (15 g) butter
1 sheet of puff pastry, thawed
4 ounces (120 g) soft goat cheese, sliced
Two 4.2-ounce (120 g) tins of sardines in olive oil, drained
½ bunch of tarragon, leaves only, coarsely chopped

1. Heat a splash of olive oil in a frying pan over medium-high heat and sauté the garlic and onion for 3 to 4 minutes, until softened. Add the leek and sauté for a further 3 to 4 minutes. Let the mixture cool a little.

2. Beat the eggs in a bowl and season with salt and pepper. Stir in the cooled leek mixture and set aside.

3. Meanwhile, heat the oven to 400°F (200°C).

4. Line a low-sided pie pan with parchment paper and melt the butter in a saucepan. Brush the sheet of puff pastry with the butter and line the pie pan with it, buttered side down, letting it overhang by ¾ inch (2 cm). Pour in the leek-egg mixture, cover with the slices of goat cheese, and top with the sardines. Sprinkle with the tarragon.

5. Tuck in the edges of the pastry and bake the pie for 20 minutes, until golden brown and done. Serve warm.

Tip: What's left of the pie is very tasty served cold for lunch or as a snack the next day!

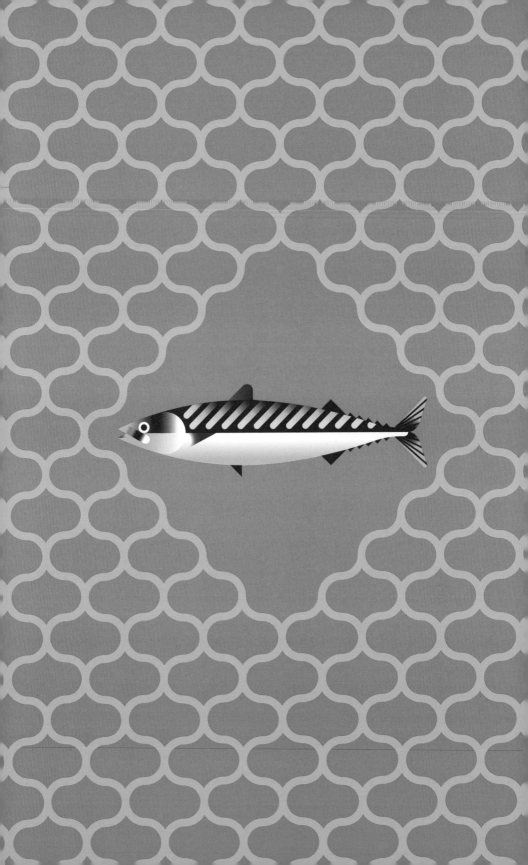

MACKEREL

SPECIES
Atlantic mackerel (Scomber scombrus)

MAXIMUM WEIGHT AND LENGTH
6.6 pounds, 2 feet long (3 kg and 60 cm)

FISHING METHODS
Pelagic trawl

MSC-CERTIFIED MACKEREL FISHERIES
*Faroese Pelagic Organisation in Klaksvik, Faroe
    Islands*
*Northern Ireland Pelagic Sustainability Group
    (NIPSG) in Fraserbrug, Scotland*
*Iceland Sustainable Fisheries (ISF) in
    Reykjavik, Iceland*

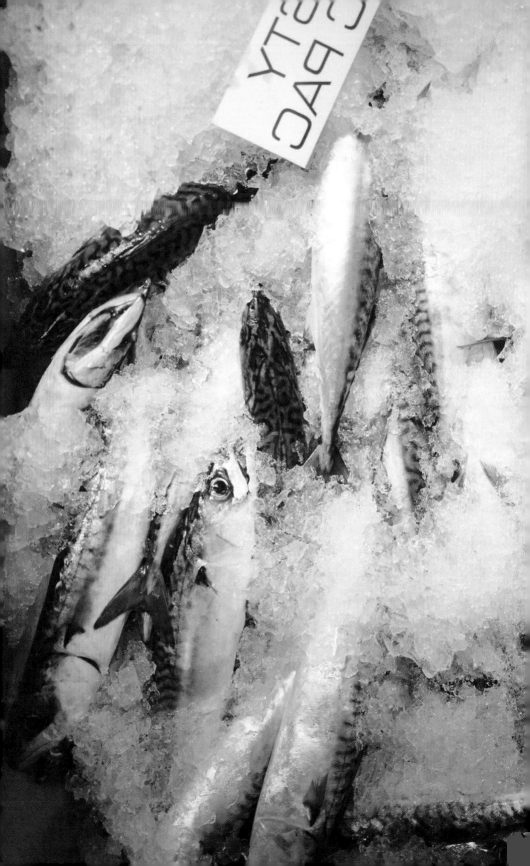

THE MIGHTY MACKEREL

Mackerel are migratory, predatory fish that swim in schools and are capable of covering large distances. The most common species—Atlantic mackerel—can be found in the North Atlantic. In winter they move into deeper waters and remain close to the seabed, fasting or eating virtually nothing. At this point, they're not at their best for consumption. In spring they head back to warmer coastal waters to spawn and fill up with food again. And that's when they're caught.

The Danish Faroe Islands, in the center of the Scotland-Norway-Iceland triangle, is a favorite hangout for mackerel. And it is on the northern-most island of Bordoy, surrounded by tall mountains, that we find the Faroese Pelagic Organisation (FPO). During the season, eleven boats with a total of three hundred hardworking fishermen set sail from the harbor of Klaksvik. Many of the men on this small island hail from fishing families, with the trade passed down from generation to generation, father to son.

These are the robust seafarers who man the FPO's pelagic trawlers. During rainy periods, especially, the driving wind and precipitation will often make for hard work for the fishermen in their thick, protective clothing. While out at sea, they use large pulleys to stretch the trawl—a cone-shaped, floating net—behind the vessel, in the middle water column. The trawl is towed through the water by the fast-moving boat, trapping the mackerel, which naturally swim in dense schools. As soon as the net is filled with fish, it's winched back on board, where the fishermen wait for the captain's signal to lower the mackerel into the ice-cold seawater in the boat's hold.

Back on shore, the mackerel are sorted by size and weight before the best ones are selected for processing. Like herring and sardines, mackerel have firm flesh and a strong flavor, so in addition to being canned in water or oil, they're often smoked or paired with sauces and other flavorings.

BOUNTIFUL MACKEREL

In many places the world over, mackerel populations are healthy. The fish are beautiful and oily, packed with nutritious omega-3 fatty acids. And there's a good reason for that. Mackerel are real gluttons. A young mackerel feeds on organisms that are found in plankton, such as small crustaceans and fish larvae. They swim through plankton concentrations with their mouths open and filter the small creatures out of the water with their gill sieve. Mature mackerel also hunt for small fish like whitebait and young herring. Super tender thanks to its hearty diet, this oily swimmer makes a delicious and affordable ingredient, be it fresh, smoked, or canned.

STARRY MACKEREL

The Faroe Islands, a group of eighteen small islands, has been home to Koks, a Michelin-starred restaurant since 2017. The highlight of its extensive menu is mackerel, a natural product that is popular not only on the islands, but in the whole of northern Europe. Plain and canned with just a bit of oil, the mackerel retains its lovely flavors and nutrients and lends itself extremely well to a classic mushroom risotto (p. 109) or a potato frittata (p. 114). The flavor intensifies if the mackerel is smoked prior to canning. This works well in our simple lentil salad (p. 106), which becomes a more substantial dish with the addition of mackerel.

SHARING IS CARING

In 2010, Scotland, Norway, Iceland, and the Faroe Islands were embroiled in a heated dispute about fishing quotas and catch shares for each country. This not only compromised mutual relations, but jeopardized fish stocks, too. The EU has since reached new agreements, and the fisheries stick to their total allowable catch to keep fish populations healthy. Since 2016 the Faroese Pelagic Organisation (FPO) has been one of the MSC-certified mackerel fisheries around the Faroes.

SMOKED MACKEREL LENTIL SALAD

►SERVES 2 AS A MAIN COURSE◄

SALAD
1 cup (200 g) lentils, preferably
   Puy
4 sprigs of parsley, 2 whole, 2 leaves
   only
1 sprig of thyme
1 garlic clove, bruised
1 bay leaf
Two 4.4-ounce (125 g) tins
   of mackerel in sunflower oil,
   drained, in chunks

½ red onion, minced
¼ yellow bell pepper, diced
Salt and pepper, to taste
Juice of 1 lemon
4 sprigs of basil, leaves only

DRESSING
2 tablespoons sherry vinegar
1 tablespoon Dijon mustard
Salt
6 to 7 tablespoons sunflower oil

1. **To make the lentils:** Place a large pan of cold, unsalted water on high heat and add the lentils, 2 sprigs of parsley, thyme, garlic, and the bay leaf. Bring to a boil, turn down the heat, and cook the lentils for 20 to 25 minutes, until al dente. Stir with a wooden spoon from time to time.

2. **To make the dressing:** Beat the vinegar, mustard, and a little salt together with a fork in a small bowl. Add the oil drop by drop, beating all the while until the dressing comes together. Add a few drops of water if the dressing is too thick.

3. Drain the lentils, remove the herbs, and let the lentils cool to lukewarm. Mix in the dressing and leave to cool further.

4. Add the mackerel chunks, red onion, and bell pepper. Combine everything well and season with salt and pepper. Drizzle with lemon juice and scatter the parsley and basil leaves on top. Serve immediately.

MACKEREL AND MUSHROOM RISOTTO

›SERVES 2 AS A MAIN COURSE‹

3 tablespoons (45 g) butter
1 shallot, minced
1 garlic clove, minced
1 cup (200 g) risotto rice (arborio
   or carnaroli)
⅔ cup (150 ml) white wine
4¼ cups (1 L) mushroom stock

1½ cups (150 g) mixed mushrooms,
   diced (preferably including oyster,
   beech, and chestnut mushrooms)
Salt and pepper, to taste
½ bunch of parsley, leaves only,
   finely chopped
Two 4.4-ounce (125 g) tins of
   mackerel in sunflower oil, drained

1. Heat 1 tablespoon of butter in a deep pan over medium-high heat and sauté the shallot and garlic for 3 to 4 minutes, until softened. Add the rice, stir-frying the grains for 2 minutes, until translucent, before adding the wine.

2. Add a soup ladle of the stock and wait for the rice to absorb most of the liquid. Keep stirring and add the next ladle of stock. Repeat until the rice is nearly done and creamy.

3. Meanwhile, add another tablespoon of butter to a frying pan and sauté the mushrooms for 3 to 5 minutes on medium-high heat.

4. Season the risotto with salt and lots of pepper. Around 2 minutes before the rice is done, add the sautéed mushrooms and half of the parsley and heat through.

5. Remove the risotto from the heat and stir in the mackerel together with the remaining tablespoon of butter. Sprinkle with the rest of the parsley and freshly ground black pepper. Serve immediately.

MACKEREL TARTE TATIN

>SERVES 2 AS A MAIN COURSE<

1 eggplant
1 medium white onion
6 tablespoons balsamic vinegar
3 tablespoons sundried tomatoes
    from a jar, drained, cut into strips

One 4.4-ounce (125 g) tin of
    mackerel in sunflower oil, drained
½ bunch of thyme, leaves only, plus
    extra
1 sheet of fresh puff pastry

1. Preheat the oven to 425°F (220°C).

2. Cut the eggplant and onion into slices around ⅕ inch (0.5 cm) thick. Put the vinegar in a small bowl and dredge the vegetables through it.

3. Spread the eggplant slices in a low pie pan and top with the onion slices, strips of tomato, and mackerel fillets. Sprinkle with the ½ bunch of thyme leaves.

4. Cover the tarte tatin with the puff pastry and, if necessary, cut off any excess dough. Bake the tarte tatin in the oven for 20 to 25 minutes, until golden brown and crusty.

5. Once slightly cool, slide a large plate over the pan and carefully—but quickly—flip it over. Serve the tarte tatin scattered with the extra thyme leaves.

Tip: Store any remaining tarte tatin in a covered container. Reheat it in the oven or eat cold the next day.

MACKEREL ASPARAGUS SALAD WITH SESAME VINAIGRETTE

>SERVES 2 AS A SIDE DISH<

SALAD

7 ounces (200 g) green asparagus,
  tough ends cut off
One 4.4-ounce (125 g) tin of
  mackerel in sunflower oil, drained
Olive oil
Salt and pepper, to taste
1 scallion, thinly sliced into rings
Handful of purple shiso leaves
  (optional)

SESAME VINAIGRETTE

2 tablespoons sunflower oil
1 tablespoon white sesame seeds
1 tablespoon black sesame seeds
3 tablespoons rice vinegar
3 tablespoons mirin
1½ tablespoons soy sauce

1. **To make the asparagus:** Place a grill pan over high heat. Brush the asparagus with some olive oil and roast for 6 to 8 minutes—turning frequently—until slightly charred in places. Let them cool a little before cutting into 1½-inch (3 to 4 cm) pieces.

2. **To make the vinaigrette:** Heat the sunflower oil in a frying pan over medium-high heat, add both types of sesame seed, and stir-fry until the seeds change color and release their fragrance. Transfer the seeds to a small bowl and leave to cool.

3. Pour the vinegar, mirin, and soy sauce into the bowl with the sesame seeds and beat with a fork until smooth. Set the dressing aside.

4. Put the green asparagus on a platter, drizzle with half of the dressing, and toss together. Break the mackerel into pieces and arrange over the asparagus salad. Drizzle with a bit more of the dressing and season with salt and pepper. Serve the asparagus topped with the scallion, shiso leaves, if using, and the rest of the dressing.

MACKEREL AND POTATO FRITTATA

›SERVES 2 AS A MAIN COURSE‹

7 ounces (200 g) Yukon Gold
  potatoes, peeled and halved
6 eggs
Scant ¼ cup (50 ml) milk
Salt and pepper, to taste
Olive oil

Two 4.4-ounce (125 g) tins of
  mackerel in sunflower oil, drained
1 handful fresh spinach, coarsely
  chopped
¾ cup (75 g) grated fontina cheese
¼ bunch of arugula, leaves only

1. Preheat the oven to 350°F (180°C).

2. Boil the potatoes in a pan with plenty of salted water until fork-tender. Let them cool a little before cutting them into slices. Set aside.

3. Whisk the eggs with the milk in a bowl, and season with salt and pepper. Mix in the potato slices until they're all thoroughly coated.

4. Heat some olive oil in an ovenproof pan over medium-high heat, pour in the potato-egg mixture, add the mackerel and press it down a little, cooking on low heat with the lid on until the egg starts to set.

5. Top the frittata with spinach, scatter the fontina on top, and season with salt and pepper. Put the pan in the oven for 5 to 7 minutes, until the spinach has wilted and the cheese has melted. Serve the frittata with arugula.

HERRING

SPECIES
Atlantic herring (Clupea harengus)

MAXIMUM WEIGHT AND LENGTH
2.5 ounces, 1.3 feet (70 g and 40 cm)

FISHING METHODS
Pelagic trawl

MSC-CERTIFIED HERRING FISHERIES
DPPO and DFPO North Sea Herring
PFA & SPSG North Sea Herring

LIKE HERRING IN A BARREL

The pride of the North Sea, the subject of many a sea shanty, and probably the least popular snack of foreign visitors to the Netherlands: raw herring. So-called *hollandse nieuwe*, or soused herring, is briny, with a very distinctive flavor—rather fishy, you might say. Although widely consumed in the Netherlands in its raw, salted state, herring is also canned and jarred.

It's not common knowledge that herring is often smoked before it's canned, which brings the flavor of the firm fish closer to that of smoked mackerel. Opening a jar of pickled herring, on the other hand, is like opening a jar of gherkins—but instead of vegetables, it contains beautiful fillets of fish with a delicious flavor as well as a long shelf life. Even after smoking or pickling, herring remains incredibly versatile in the kitchen.

Those who are curious to know which kind of herring is suitable for which method of processing—and decide to google it—will find all kinds of "expert advice" on the web. So which herring ends up in a can? And which in a jar? And which variety do the Dutch like to eat raw?

HERRING IS . . . HERRING

The Dutch are particularly fond of soused herring. The oily fish is usually bought at the market or a street stall and devoured with chopped raw onion on the side—often using a little Dutch toothpick flag.

Provided the circumstances are right, herring is caught in the North Sea between May 1 and August 31. The fish that becomes soused herring is caught when it has reached sexual maturity but hasn't yet developed any soft (in the case of the male) or hard (in the case of the female) roe, and preferably before a quarter of its body weight consists of fat. This usually happens in the months of June and July. This oily herring can only be called hollandse nieuwe if it's gutted in the traditional way (which involves the removal of the gill arches and part of the gullet), cured, and matured.

The herring that's smoked and canned or pickled and jarred is the exact same species, but it's been caught either earlier or later than the soused variety. That means it's not quite as rich and oily. But whatever the processing technique, the fish must all be frozen right after catch in order to prevent herring worm.

HOW DO YOU LIKE YOURS?

All countries that fish for herring have their own distinct way of preparing and consuming it. Did you know that in Denmark pickled herring is eaten with a mustard and curry sauce? Even more unusual, next door in Sweden they like their herring fermented. People in the Netherlands have slightly different tastes. Smoked herring from a tin is an excellent accompaniment to traditional Dutch *hete bliksem*, literally "hot lightning," a mashed potato dish that also contains stewed apples (p. 124). Pickled herring from a jar calls for strong supporting flavors. Think of horseradish, apple, and capers in a delicious potato salad (p. 127)—with or without a cocktail stick with a small flag.

HERRING GALORE

Soused, tinned, and jarred herring may be caught at different times of the year, but the fishing method is always the same: pelagic trawls.

A trawl is a cone-shaped, floating net that's suspended in the middle water column behind a herring vessel. The boat's propulsion then tows the net through the water. Herring naturally swim in very dense shoals. Fishermen can locate these with the help of sonar equipment and draw the net selectively around them. The trawls have been designed in such a way that small, young herring can escape through the mesh.

As soon as the net is full, it's hauled on board. The herring then goes straight into the chilled seawater in the boat's hold, where it remains super fresh. Upon arrival in the harbor, the fish is pumped directly from the ship into the processing plant. Depending on its purpose, the herring is cleaned, gutted, or filleted, and finally frozen.

Not all herring sold and consumed in the US is necessarily MSC-certified—which, of course, would guarantee that the fish was caught sustainably from well-managed and healthy fish stocks. So just remember: When buying herring in a tin or jar, it's advisable to carefully check the label.

SMOKED HERRING SHAKSHUKA

Olive oil
1 medium yellow onion, finely diced
2 garlic cloves, minced
1 red bell pepper, in strips
1 yellow bell pepper, in strips
½ red chile, seeded and finely
  chopped
One 14-ounce (400 g) can chopped
  tomatoes

2 tablespoons harissa
2 teaspoons tomato purée
1 teaspoon cumin powder
4 eggs
One 6.7-ounce (198 g) tin of
  smoked herring, drained
Salt and pepper, to taste
Zest of ½ lemon
Cilantro leaves, to taste

1. Heat a dash of olive oil in a frying pan with a lid over medium-high heat and sauté the onion, garlic, peppers, and chile for 3 to 4 minutes, until softened.

2. Add the chopped tomato, harissa, tomato purée, and cumin and cook for 15 minutes on low heat.

3. Make four indentations in the sauce and crack an egg in each hollow. Arrange the herring fillets around it, cover with the lid, and let the eggs set in 10 minutes. Season with salt and pepper, scatter the lemon zest on top, and serve with plenty of cilantro.

Tip: You can use smoked mackerel instead of smoked herring, if you'd like!

DUTCH MASH WITH SMOKED HERRING

➤SERVES 2 AS A MAIN COURSE◄

½ pound (300 g) russet potatoes, halved

1½ cup (150 g) cooking apples (such as Rome), cored and diced

1½ cup (150 g) sweet apples (such as Gala), cored and diced

Salt and pepper, to taste

6 tablespoons (90 g) butter, cut into small pieces

1 onion, diced

½ cup (100 ml) whole milk

One 6.7-ounce (198 g) tin of smoked herring, drained, cut into chunks

1 scallion, thinly sliced into rings

1. Place the potatoes in a large stockpot and top them with the diced apple. Add enough water to just cover everything, add salt, and bring to a boil over high heat. Cook for 15 to 20 minutes, until done.

2. Meanwhile, heat 1 tablespoon of butter in a frying pan over medium-high heat and sauté the onion until soft and translucent. Set aside.

3. Drain the potatoes and apples and add the onion and the milk. Season with salt and pepper. Mash everything with a potato masher until it reaches the fine or coarse texture you prefer. Top the warm mash with the herring and replace the lid to keep the potato-apple mixture hot and to allow the herring to warm through.

4. Melt the rest of the butter in a pan, stirring continuously. After around 30 seconds it will start bubbling and foaming. Keep stirring until the butter begins to color, but be careful not to let it burn. Pour the browned butter into a small bowl.

5. Divide the Dutch mash between two plates and top each portion with a few pieces of herring fillet. Serve with a splash of browned butter and a sprinkle of scallion.

POTATO AND HERRING SALAD

>SERVES 2 AS A STARTER OR SIDE DISH<

SALAD
1½ cups (240 g) baby potatoes
4 rollmops herring fillets, from a jar
   (save the liquid)
2 Granny Smith apples, peeled
   and thinly sliced (sprinkled
   with lemon juice to prevent
   discoloring)
1 small red onion, thinly sliced into
   rings

2 tablespoons capers
½ bunch of dill, finely chopped
Salt and pepper, to taste

DRESSING
2 teaspoons horseradish
2 tablespoons crème fraîche
2 tablespoons mayonnaise
Salt and pepper, to taste
Worcestershire sauce, to taste

1. **To make the potatoes:** Boil the baby potatoes in plenty of salted water until fork-tender. Drain them in a colander and allow them to cool to lukewarm before cutting them in half.

2. **To make the dressing:** Combine the horseradish, crème fraîche, and mayonnaise in a bowl and stir through 1 tablespoon of the herring liquid. Season with salt, pepper, and some Worcestershire sauce. Set aside.

3. Cut the herring fillets diagonally into 1¼-inch (3 cm) pieces and set aside. Mix the baby potatoes, apple, red onion, capers, and nearly all the dill in a large bowl and add most of the dressing. Stir until all of the ingredients are coated and season with salt and pepper.

4. Divide the potato salad between two plates, top each portion with a few strips of herring, and serve with an extra splash of dressing and the remaining dill.

CRAB, COD LIVER, MUSSELS, AND MORE

SPOILS FROM THE WORLD'S OCEANS

Walk into a random supermarket in southern Europe and you'll be amazed by the extensive selection of tinned fish products. While North American shops usually have only a shelf or two with tuna, salmon, anchovies, and sardines, the Mediterranean sun worshippers pull out all the stops with wall-to-wall tinned fish. The packaging boasts splendid illustrations of squid, razor clams, oysters, and octopus. And that's not to mention the alluring, brightly colored wrappers that turn these tins into culinary souvenirs. Tins are popular here—and no wonder. Compared to fresh fish, seafood in tins is more affordable and therefore more accessible to many people. Provided that it's processed in a good cannery, the delicious flavors and wholesome nutrients will be preserved so you can have top quality in your cupboard.

BACK IN TIME

In the old days, cod and haddock liver were dinnertime staples, but they've become a lot less popular these days. Such a shame! Fish liver is incredibly healthy—the offal contains exceptionally high levels of vitamin A and D, and more omega-3 than any other part of the fish. And it's tasty, too. The high fat content makes it a very filling ingredient, though, so use it in moderation. The recipe for Cod Liver with Miso and Herring (p. 132) shows you how it's done!

LIKE A NEEDLE IN A HAYSTACK

In the US it can be quite a challenge to find sustainably sourced crab, cod liver, mussels, or cockles in a tin or jar. If you can't locate some of these harder-to-find ingredients in stores, many are often available online, and specialist stores can help, too. Always check to see if the fish and crustaceans carry the MSC certification label, so you know they were caught sustainably in the wild.

COD LIVER WITH MISO AND HERRING

›SERVES 2 AS A STARTER‹

One 4.3-ounce (120 g) tin of cod
  liver, drained
1 tablespoon miso paste
1 teaspoon Dijon mustard
1 tablespoon powdered sugar
1 tablespoon rice vinegar
4 teaspoons mirin

2 teaspoons dry sake
2 pickled herring fillets, from a jar,
  cut into pieces
1 scallion, thinly sliced
1 teaspoon pink peppercorns
Small handful shiso leaves
  (optional)

1. Heat the cod liver in a saucepan over low heat and while stirring let it "melt"—the liver will slowly disintegrate.

2. Put the miso paste in a large mortar, add the melted cod liver, and with a pestle grind the two together into a thick paste.

3. Add the mustard, mix with the pestle, and then stir in the powdered sugar. Pour the vinegar, mirin, and sake into the mortar and combine everything into a smooth purée. Finally, press the liver-miso paste through a fine sieve.

4. Divide the paste between two plates and top each portion with several pieces of herring, scallion, and a few peppercorns. Serve with the shiso leaves, if using.

CRAB AND FENNEL WATERCRESS SALAD

►SERVES 2 AS A STARTER OR SIDE DISH◄

2 tablespoons pine nuts
¼ cup (50 ml) orange juice
2 tablespoons mayonnaise
Zest of ½ lime
One 6-ounce (170 g) tin of crabmeat, drained
Salt and pepper, to taste
2¼ cup (80 g) watercress or arugula
1 fennel bulb, cleaned, thinly sliced, green fronds saved
1 orange, peeled, cut into segments
4 radishes, sliced
Cayenne pepper, to taste

1. Heat a frying pan over medium-high heat and dry-roast the pine nuts until golden brown, about 3 to 4 minutes. Set aside.

2. Combine the orange juice, mayonnaise, and lime zest and mix in the crabmeat. Season with salt and pepper and set aside.

3. Divide the watercress, fennel slices, and orange segments between two plates. Spoon on the crabmeat, scatter the radish slices and roasted pine nuts on top, and dust with cayenne pepper.

CRAB FALAFEL WITH LABNEH AND SEA VEGETABLE SALAD

>SERVES 2 AS A STARTER OR SNACK<

LABNEH
Scant 2 cups (½ L) full-fat yogurt
½ tablespoon salt
Extra virgin olive oil
1 tablespoon za'atar

FALAFEL
Half a 14-ounce (400 g) can of
 chickpeas, drained
One 6-ounce (170 g) tin of
 crabmeat, drained
1 tablespoon ras el hanout

½ bunch of cilantro, leaves only,
 coarsely chopped, plus extra
Zest of 1 lemon, plus extra wedges
½ teaspoon baking powder
2 tablespoons all-purpose flour
Salt and pepper, to taste
Sunflower oil

SEA VEGETABLE SALAD
4 cups (200 g) sea vegetables
 (wakame, kombu, etc.)
Juice of ½ lemon
Olive oil

1. **To make the labneh:** Line a sieve with a clean dish towel or cheesecloth and suspend the sieve above a fitting bowl, making sure the bottom of the sieve doesn't touch that of the bowl. Pour the yogurt into the cloth and either tie it at the top or cover the yogurt with a clean plate. Leave it in the fridge overnight.

2. **To make the falafel:** Combine the chickpeas, crabmeat, ras el hanout, cilantro, lemon zest, baking powder, and the flour in a food processor and season with salt and pepper. Process into a stiff dough, cover with plastic wrap, and leave to firm up in the fridge for 30 minutes.

3. **To make the salad:** Bring a pot of water to a boil and blanch the sea vegetables for 30 seconds. Drain and add the lemon juice, a dash of olive oil, salt, and pepper. Set aside.

4. Shape the falafel dough into balls the size of a golf ball and flatten them a little. Heat a generous layer of sunflower oil in a thick-bottomed pan and fry the falafels in stages until golden brown, about 4 to 6 minutes for each falafel. Flip them regularly to ensure even cooking. Lift the falafels out of the oil with a skimmer and let them drain on kitchen paper. Repeat until all of the dough has been used up.

5. Meanwhile, take the yogurt out of the fridge, pour out the sour fluid at the bottom of the bowl, and mix the thick labneh with the salt. Transfer to a dish, drizzle with olive oil, and sprinkle with za'atar.

6. Serve the falafel with the labneh, sea vegetable salad, extra cilantro, and a slice of lemon.

Tip: Any remaining labneh will keep in the fridge for 2 to 4 days.

THAI RICE SOUP WITH MUSSELS AND WAKAME

►SERVES 2 AS A MAIN COURSE◄

Olive oil, to taste
1 teaspoon shrimp paste
1 garlic clove, minced
2 scallions, sliced diagonally into
   rings
½-inch (1 cm) piece of ginger,
   peeled and finely chopped
1 cup (150 g) cooked rice (such as
   Jasmine or Basmati)
2 cups (500 ml) seafood stock
¼ cup (6 g) dried wakame

2 eggs, hardboiled and peeled
1 tablespoon fish sauce
2 tablespoons soy sauce, plus extra
½ cup (50 g) bean sprouts
Generous ½ cup (100 g) edamame,
   peeled
One 12.3-ounce (350 g) tin or jar
   of mussels, drained*
½ bunch of cilantro, leaves only,
   coarsely chopped

1. Heat a splash of olive oil in a soup pan over medium-high heat and sauté the shrimp paste, garlic, half of the scallion, and the ginger for 3 to 4 minutes, until soft. Pour in the stock and simmer while you prepare the other ingredients.

2. Meanwhile, add the wakame to a bowl with 2 cups (½ L) of hot water and let it rehydrate for 10 minutes. Drain the seaweed in a colander for 5 minutes and cut into ¾-inch (2 cm) pieces before leaving them to cool.

3. Heat a layer of olive oil to 350°F (180°C). Fry the eggs in the oil until they have a pale golden crust. Lift the eggs out of the pan with a slotted spoon and let them drain on paper towels.

4. Add the rice to the soup and season with the fish sauce and soy sauce. Add most of the bean sprouts, edamame, mussels, and wakame and heat through.

5. Divide the rice soup between two bowls and serve each portion with the rest of the bean sprouts and scallion, cilantro, and fried eggs, halved.

*Note: If you can't find mussels, two 6.5-ounce cans of chopped clams will also do!

TUNA AND CAPER BUTTER

➤SERVES 2 AS A STARTER OR SNACK◄

*One 5-ounce (140 g) tin of tuna in
  olive oil, drained
¼ shallot, minced*

*5 tablespoons (75 g) butter
1 teaspoon capers
Salt and pepper, to taste*

1. Put all the ingredients in a food processor and season with salt and pepper. Combine to form a smooth spread.

2. Transfer the tuna and caper butter to a small dish, cover with plastic wrap, and leave to firm up in the fridge for at least 1 hour.

ANCHOVY AND OLIVE SPREAD

➤SERVES 2 AS A STARTER OR SNACK◄

*Half a 2-ounce (45 g) tin of
  anchovies, drained
1 cup (100 g) Taggiasca olives,
  pitted
½ garlic clove, minced*

*¼ bunch of thyme, leaves only
Juice of ½ lemon
Olive oil
Salt and pepper, to taste*

Put all the ingredients in a food processor together with a splash of olive oil and season with salt and pepper. Combine into a coarse spread, adding some extra olive oil if the texture is too thick.

MACKEREL SALAD

One 4.4-ounce (125 g) tin of
   smoked mackerel, drained
1 tablespoon crème fraîche
½ tablespoon capers
¼ bunch of chives, finely chopped
Zest and juice of ½ lemon

Salt and pepper, to taste
Toasted bread
Cornichons, to serve
Pickled onions, to serve (recipe
   follows)

1. Put the mackerel fillets into a bowl and tear the meat apart with two forks. Mix the fish with the crème fraîche, capers, chives, lemon zest and juice, and season with salt and pepper.

2. Serve the mackerel salad with toast, cornichons, and onions.

PICKLED ONIONS

►SERVES 2 AS A STARTER, SNACK, OR SIDE DISH◄

½ pound (250 g) fresh pearl or
   cocktail onions
½ cup (100 ml) balsamic vinegar
½ cup (100 ml) white vinegar

⅛ cup (25 g) cane sugar
1 teaspoon salt
1 teaspoon caraway seeds
1 clean preserving jar

1. Put the onions in a pan or a bowl, with their skins still on. Add enough water to cover them and some salt. Leave the onions overnight.

2. Peel the onions and set aside. Put both vinegars, the cane sugar, 1 teaspoon of salt, and the caraway seeds into a pan and bring to a boil. Reduce the heat and boil down for 4 minutes. Add the peeled onions and cook for a further 12 to 14 minutes, until the onions are soft. Scoop them out of the vinegar with a slotted spoon and transfer to the preserving jar. Next, pour in the vinegar from the pan until the onions are completely covered.

3. Store the jar in a dark place for at least 2 weeks, but preferably longer, until ready for use. Serve with a selection of fish appetizers.

ACKNOWLEDGMENTS

I'm incredibly proud of another beautiful book. I've loved working with you all. Thank you!

David Loftus, this is the fourth book we've made together. Many thanks for the photography. Thank you, Inge Tichelaar, for the terrific styling and production. Eline Cox, thank you for your support! It feels like we've been doing this for years. Thank you for your beautiful turns of phrase and your immense dedication.

My thanks to Tijs Koelemeijer for yet another gorgeous layout and to Wouter Eertink for the sleek design.

The Experiment Publishing and Julia Foldenyi, thank you so much for bringing my book into the US and Canada. So exciting! And thank you so much Liana Willis, Laura Vroomen, and Jennifer Hergenroeder for your fantastic work.

I'd also like to thank all at Kosmos Uitgevers, and especially Claire Schalm, Melanie Zwartjes, and Bert Zuidhof. My thanks to Lars Hamer for the culinary editing and Kirsten Verhagen for her editing work.

Thank you, Daan de Rooij, for your help with the cooking. And the entire Fish Tales team: Thank you for your support.

Dear Bo, Juul, and Ties, thank you for your support and patience. Love you!

Last but not least, my thanks to all the fishermen and women who make sure that we get to enjoy the tastiest tinned fish, now and in the future.

ABOUT THE AUTHOR

BART VAN OLPHEN is arguably the world's most passionate sustainable fishing advocate and overall lover of fish: He was named "world's most sustainable seafood entrepreneur" in 2008, and his book *Fish Tales: Stories & Recipes from Sustainable Fisheries Around the World* won the 2011 Gourmand World Cookbook Award for "best sustainable cookbook." He is also the cofounder of the tinned fish brand Fish Tales. You can check out his travels around the world and enjoy his cooking show on Instagram (@bartsfishtales) and YouTube (featured on Jamie Oliver's FoodTube Network)—and at fish-tales.com.